WHY FAITH MATTERS

WHY
FAITH
MATTERS

DAVID J. WOLPE

HarperOne
An Imprint of HarperCollins Publishers

HarperOne

Grateful acknowledgement is made to Houghton Mifflin Harcourt Publishers for permission to print "Choruses from the Rock" from T. S. Eliot, *Collected Poems 1909–1962.*

HarperCollins books may be purchased for educational, business, or sales promotional use. For information, please write: Special Markets Department, HarperCollins Publishers, 10 East 53rd Street, New York, NY 10022.

HarperCollins Web site: http://www.harpercollins.com
HarperCollins®, 📖 ®, and HarperOne™ are
trademarks of HarperCollins Publishers

FIRST EDITION

Designed by Level C

Library of Congress Cataloging-in-Publication Data is available upon request.
ISBN 978–0–06–163334–8

08 09 10 11 12   RRD   10 9 8 7 6 5 4 3 2 1

For Eliana and Samara:
All the proof I need.

CONTENTS

FOREWORD

THIS BEAUTIFUL BOOK is a gift to all of us. So much of what is published today about faith just rehashes warmed-over clichés and feels out of touch with reality. In contrast, every page of this special volume has the smell of authenticity on it.

My dear friend, Rabbi David Wolpe, has written a candid and captivating account of how his personal journey of faith began with doubt. Spurred on by the current movement of "new atheism," David humbly set out to re-examine his own struggles of faith by asking himself a myriad of questions. Those very questions ultimately brought him back to the bedrock of faith in God.

David passionately believes, as I do, that science and religion can and should be productive partners in the search for meaning and truth. In many ways, this book reinforces Einstein's famous quote: "Science without religion is lame; religion without science is blind."

The major age-old tensions are covered here: religion causing violence, religion being disproved by science, whether religion makes you happy, what religion actually teaches, and other vital issues. David's answers are refreshingly direct and thought-provoking, and he draws from a myriad of sources: classic literature, philosophy, science, and from many of the great minds throughout history. I particularly admire his thoughtful and courageous response to both Darwinian fundamentalism and religious fanaticism.

The closer I get to David Wolpe, the more I am impressed by this man of faith. As an author, religious teacher, professor, cancer victim, and television commentator, his unique combination of experiences has given him a credible platform from which he presents the case that faith in God truly matters at this critical time in our world.

Regardless of where you are on your own personal faith journey, I'm certain that the profound insights in this book will stimulate your thinking and even touch your soul about the reality of God in fresh and surprising ways.

Dr. Rick Warren
The Purpose-Driven Life
Saddleback Church

PRELUDE

I STOOD BY the hospital bed of a friend who was dying of cancer. Isaac wanted to know why he was sick, why he must die, why he must leave his children and grandchildren. I could tell him that it was part of God's plan or confess to him that I did not know. Neither response seemed right.

So instead, we exchanged stories about chemotherapy. My hair was just beginning to grow back after a bout with lymphoma; Isaac's, wispy to start, was gone from the drugs that had targeted all the fast-growing cells in his body. They had done a thorough job on his hair but not on his cancer.

We talked about the strange gratitude we felt for the medicinal poison as it coursed through our veins. There was a moment of solidarity, and then sadness returned. Battle stories are not nostalgic when they end in death.

"But at least you understand," Isaac said. It reminded me anew that in many ways my cancer was a gift; it gave more context to my compassion. He knew that I really did understand, that my family and I were not unscathed. Needles seemed forever to be dangling from my arm and I was always being shoved into metal tubes for scans and pictures and tests. Enduring the survival machines creates a kind of tribal solidarity.

"So," he asked, "why did it happen to you?"

Did I get cancer for a reason? Four years before my lymphoma I had undergone surgery for a brain tumor, thankfully benign. Five years before that, after the birth of our daughter, my wife's cancer led to surgery that cured her but left her unable to bear more children. After each experience, people would ask why it happened and what I learned. Now someone was asking not out of curiosity or even spiritual hunger, but existential urgency.

We looked at each other for a long time. I felt the familiar fear—that shiver inside that began with diagnosis and will never leave. I gathered myself and answered as best I could:

I know what it does not mean, I told Isaac. It is not a punishment. The calculus of reward and punishment in this world is surely more complex than sin equals cancer. In my darkest moments when I was most afraid I still did not believe God decreed I would get cancer because I had not lived up to expectations. Isaac, I said to him, the cancer is bad enough without making yourself feel guilty for it.

One thing more is clear, I continued: The cancer is not only about you. Those who care for you suffer as well. The ripples do not end. Perhaps it is also about what you will bring to those who come to you for comfort.

Facing our own mortality, the traditional roles had melted away. We were no longer clergy and layperson, younger man and older man. The first verse of the Book of Kings reads: "Now King David was old" (1 Kings 1:1). One chapter later, his condition has declined: "Now the days of David drew near that he should die" (1 Kings 2:1). Approaching death, he is no longer King David, just David. No one faces death as a king, a doctor, or a preacher. Death strips away pretense. There is no hiding behind titles and status. Isaac and I were two people who had undergone similar ailments. One of us, for now, was in remission, and one of us would die before the other. And neither knew why.

He told me that he feared not for himself but for the fate of his family. How would they cope with losing him? I remembered my own surprise a few years before as I was wheeled into surgery, at how little I feared death. I feared instead the consequences of my death—what it would mean to my wife and my daughter. It terrified me to leave them alone.

Did he believe in another world? He was not sure, but he hoped. I ventured that everything a human being was—the hopes and dreams, the love and gifts—could not completely disappear. As the writer Vladimir Nabokov once said, life is such a remarkable surprise, why should death be less of a surprise?

He smiled and in that smile was both sadness and a shared moment of hope. Maybe all the chemotherapy, the scans and shots, that kept us in this world were postponing the bliss of a life to come.

And yet. To die is to lose everything we know, all the wonders of this world and the people in it. To die is to leave so many stories unfinished and to miss the next act of the stories of others, those whom we know and whom we love. I felt the shiver anew as I looked into Isaac's eyes and wondered, what else can I say to him, to myself?

One thought might promise some consolation: When I was sick it became clear to me how carefully others watched my reaction—would my faith help me at all, they wondered? Does a professional practice of faith offer some strength? In sickness we are not powerless. We still have the ability to teach. I learned this from my congregation.

I told this man, my friend Isaac, that his children and grandchildren were watching him. Here was a chance to teach his greatest lesson. They would remember much about him to be sure, but they would never forget how he died. His acceptance, his dignity, even his hope, could change their lives.

Each week, I told him, I study scripture with a man who just turned ninety. He had often recounted what his mother said to him as she was dying: "My child, do not be afraid. It is only death, and it has happened to everyone who ever lived." A long lifetime later, his mother's words still bring him comfort and courage.

The two of us in the hospital room held hands, and agreed that if we could, we would pass from this life with words of love and hope for awakenings to come. Shortly afterward, Isaac passed away. His children speak of him with reverence for his life and for the way in which he faced death. As with all meetings of the spirit there was not one who gave and one who took; there were two who stood with each other and before God, and even in their sadness, felt blessed.

I REMEMBERED THAT encounter and others like it as I was writing this book. Such meetings are the deepest current of faith. Conversations I have had with people in troubled times are not marred by the narrow certainties that lead to viciousness and violence, or the smugness that often characterizes arguments against faith.

This book was begun to present the case for faith. As with so many believers, I am disturbed by the charges of the new atheism and horrified by the cruelty of a brand of fanatical faith that breeds terrorists. I do not believe our choice is either an absence of God or an over-zealous embrace of God. Every day I see and hear individuals trying to make sense of their lives, seeking the comfort of community and an assurance of the reality of God's love.

What follows is about faith and history, faith and science, faith and the way it functions in the world. Underneath all the exploration lies those ultimate questions of wonder and anguish: What awaits me after I die? What do I transmit to my children? Why are we here? Can I believe that we all live in the presence of God?

———— ◆ ————

ONE

From Faith to Doubt

*If the only prayer you ever say in your entire life is thank
you, it is sufficient.*

Meister Eckhart

DO ALL PEOPLE, in the dark of a sleepless night, wonder
if they made the right choice with their lives? No matter
what choices we make, the world brings us to unexpected
places. When I counsel young people they often tell me the
types of people they wish to marry. They come to my office
armed with checklists. No corporate recruiter could be
more thorough or thoughtful. In a year or two they return
with partners who do not match the checklists but who
have captured their hearts: "She's everything I ever wanted."
Sometimes it seems that a plan is a useful illusion until life
figures out where you really should be headed.

"Life is lived forward," Kierkegaard wrote, "but can only
be understood backward." In high school and through col-

lege I had a checklist for life—things I planned to accomplish, things I planned to avoid. Growing up in the house
of a rabbi, I wanted to avoid the responsibility of caring for
a community because I saw how burdensome it could be.
I wanted to avoid proclaiming God to the world because I
had long since ceased believing in God. I wanted to avoid
spending my life studying faith because I was convinced
that it was an illusion, and a dangerous one at that.

I can trace, but still do not fully understand, the way in
which life, or God, tossed out my checklist. And now I find
myself in love with something beautiful, something mysterious, and something completely unexpected. As with so
many things in life, the story begins in loss.

―――

MY JOURNEY TO faith was first a journey *from* faith.
Having been raised with belief, I soon came to doubt everything I had been taught. At the age of eleven, certain that
God was in His heaven and all was right with the world,
nothing seemed to threaten a settled world view. By the
time I was twelve, and for a decade after, I had lost that
faith, and everything that was once certain seemed foolish
and empty.

―――

THIRTY-TWO MINUTES SHATTERED my comfortable
world.

A short documentary was released some ten years after the end of World War II. *Night and Fog* contains profoundly disturbing footage of the liberated concentration camps and emphasizes the indifference of the world in the face of the greatest atrocities in history.

I was a twelve-year-old at summer camp when my age group gathered for the movie. The image that shocked me into disbelief was of corpses bulldozed into huge holes in the ground. These were once living human beings, mothers and children and siblings and grandparents; now they were piles of inert flesh, pushed into the unforgiving earth by machine. Spirit suddenly drained from the world. Surely, if there was a God, this would not be permitted. I walked out after seeing that movie onto the green sloping field of the camp and looked down at the lake, convinced there was no God. I was soon to find someone whose words made my conviction many times stronger.

Losing faith is not a discovery that a proposition, once believed, has proved to be false. You may find out that a medicine does not really work or a relative whom you remember fondly is actually mean-spirited. These are nasty shocks to the system, but not like losing one's faith.

"I believe in God" is not the same as "I believe in a good education." Faith is where we stand in the universe, not an idea that is checked off in the truth-or-illusion column. Losing one's faith is stepping off the planet to find oneself spinning in a new orbit.

———

IN THIS NEW orbit I needed a guide. I had been introduced to evil and a world without God's protection. Life was suddenly murky, a place of night and fog. Human life was an accident and everything that happened was a simple product of blind forces. I longed for help in navigating this new terrain. How does one live in a chaotic world? I found a path in the words of an English philosopher.

Bertrand Russell was a leading figure in twentieth-century philosophy. His unbelief was not gentle, but scathing, witty, and angry. The bitterness of Russell's tone may be partly a result of personal history. Orphaned young, he was reared by his grandmother. She gave him a religious education, successfully evading a provision in his parents' will that he be raised to be agnostic. Despite his grandmother's intervention, Russell more than lived up to his late parents' wishes. He thought religion foolish and hateful.

Russell wrote on religion with the same certainty that he brought to all questions, from the proper raising of children to pacifism. His sentences are marked by a lucid wit and a world view that seems beyond small human prejudice. Sitting in my room in high school, a chessboard on one side of the desk and a shelf of Russell's works on the other, I read him by lamplight hour after hour. His was the voice from Olympus.

Russell cast a spell of clear, calm logic. Here was the genuine scientific world view. "The whole conception of God is a conception derived from ancient Oriental despotisms. It is a conception quite unworthy of free men. When you hear people in church debasing themselves and saying they are miserable sinners, it seems contemptible and not worthy of self-respecting human beings. We ought to stand up and look the world frankly in the face. We ought to make the best we can of the world, and if it is not so good as we wish, after all it will still be better than what these others have made of it in all these ages. A good world needs knowledge, kindliness, and courage; it does not need a regretful hankering after the past, or a fettering of the free intelligence by the words uttered long ago by ignorant men."

For a high school student, this was a declaration of independence. Here was a place to stand. This was the platform of the rational and the free. I understood (for I was seventeen and understood everything) that some weak creatures would need faith. I knew that belief could buoy a crippled spirit. But I stood, along with my mentor, at the barricade of enlightened thought. Part of the attraction of atheism, especially for the young, is its sheen of bravery.

One day I was sitting on my bunk at summer camp reading Russell when one of the camp rabbis strolled by. He asked me what I was reading, and I said, defiantly and ready for an argument, "Bertrand Russell" (I was *always* reading Bertrand Russell). "Good," he said, to my amazement. "Why do you say good?" I asked, thinking perhaps he knew nothing of Russell or his views.

"David, how old are you?"

"Seventeen."

"Well, I'd rather have you grow out of him than grow into him."

———

HE PROVED IN the end to be right. My young mind was in thrall to Russell. Then I read something of his life.

Russell won the Nobel Prize for literature. His autobiography is a masterpiece; it demonstrates all of the wit, clarity, and reason for which his prose is famous. But it also shows, and later biographies of Russell amplify this, that his life was a shambles. Four marriages, proudly proclaimed infidelities, estrangement from his children: This man, who was often courageous in the public sphere and so clear in his writings, was personally a mess. I was young and did not yet know that a person in the pages of a book often bears little relation to the person one meets in the flesh. I began to understand that the clarity Russell preached was not always his. It was better to be Russell's reader than his wife or child. Could his crystalline doctrine be a nice theory, and a lousy prescription for living? He was not just another man in the street; he was the best example of reason I knew. Yet his life was strewn with the wreckage of those who loved him.

———

SUDDENLY I FOUND myself in the position of so many young people who come to me today for counseling. If faith is an illusion and reason does not teach one how to live, what is left? I remember the desolation of concluding that there was no reliable guide and no certain path. Religion was self-deception, and Russell proved to me that philosophers made their lives into the same horrid muddle as everyone else.

I made my way to an Ivy League university where the professors thought religion was inane (one told me it was "ok for people who didn't know how to think"). But my professors never presented themselves as guides to life. Lectures on philosophy or the history of literature entertained all sorts of questions, but never the question Socrates put at the center of his world, "How should one live?" Classes were a way to study how other people answered questions that we were not to ask ourselves.

I traveled, read books, argued late into the night with friends in rooms littered with beer bottles and candy wrappers. I took a cross-country bus and looked out over the Colorado Rockies and wondered if there was an invisible sculpting hand that shaped those magnificent peaks. On the ride I was offered a life fishing in Alaska or farming in Iowa. But I was not looking for an occupation; I was looking for a world that made sense. Day after day I talked to my fellow travelers and looked out the window. The universe remained mute, or if there was a voice I did not hear it.

––––––

IT IS MORE than thirty years since I took that bus ride. In that time, life threw out my checklist and brought me to a place I would not have anticipated: to my current position as a clergyman who leads a congregation, writing and speaking daily about faith. Lately there have been a number of bestselling works proclaiming, even celebrating, atheism. When I read them part of me feels yes, I know this, my soul has been in this place. I recognize it as familiar ground. I have felt anger at God's absence. I too see kind and faithful people suffer. I too see people who claim to love God but act in hateful ways.

Russell proved in the end to be an unexpectedly useful guide. The atheistic philosopher with his corrosive wit taught me to question, constantly and repeatedly. What Russell did not teach was that questions could themselves lead to faith. A brittle faith fears questions; a robust faith welcomes them.

NO QUESTIONS?

*A man may be a heretic in the truth; and if he believes
things only because his pastor says so, or the assembly so*

*determines, without knowing any other reason, though
his belief be true, yet the very truth he holds becomes his
heresy.*

Milton, *Areopagitica*

FAITH BEGINS WITH a question, the first question in the
Bible. In the garden, God asks Adam, "Where are you?"
This is a question addressed to each of us at every instant,
at all times.

The Bible answers the first question with the second. The
second question in the Bible is asked in the aftermath of
murder. When Cain kills Abel, God asks of Cain, "Where
is your brother?" We find out where we are, the first question, by discovering whether we care for others, the second
question. Cain's response to God is also, revealingly, a question: "Am I my brother's keeper?" Though he intends the
answer to be "no," it is a question that we understand needs
to be answered "yes."

Russell's mockery was intended to subvert faith and end
the discussion. Instead I pursued the questions he raised:
Because religion is ancient, must it therefore be outdated?
Is it possible for an entity to exist that cannot be seen or
measured?

There are questions that open the heart and questions
that close it. "Oh yeah?" closes it down—it is not even a
true question. "How can I understand this?" is a question.
"Will I have the strength to go through this?" is a question,

one of the deepest a human being can ask. "Doubt," as the theologian Paul Tillich wrote, "isn't the opposite of faith; it is an element of faith."

WHAT DOES IT MEAN
TO BE RELIGIOUS?

PART OF WHAT kept me from God was the assumption that I understood what religion was. To ask, "Am I religious?" presupposes that one understands what it is to feel God and to have faith. In fact, the question, properly asked, is an invitation to a journey, not an answer.

I began to ask myself questions about faith that I have, in subsequent years, asked thousands of lecture audiences:

1. Do you believe only that which is tangible—that which you can see or touch or measure—is real, or do you believe there is an intangible reality?

2. Do you believe that there is a mystery at the heart of the universe that we will never be able to fully understand, not through lack of effort but because it cannot be understood?

The first question is about scientific or philosophical materialism. We know that the world contains much that we cannot see with the naked eye—cells, atoms, molecules, the ephemeral quarks of modern physics. But all of them are in some way measurable, tangible. They exist in the physical realm. They may be measured through the space they leave behind, as a child holds his hand against a wall and sprays paint so that when he steps back the outline of a hand is visible. Particles may only suggest their presence or even change when we observe them, but still, they exist in the world.

For a religious person, there is an unseeable order, an intangible reality. Obviously such an order cannot be measured. Detection will never be possible, even with more refined instruments. When Khrushchev declared in a speech to the Soviet plenum that cosmonaut Yuri Gagarin flew into space but didn't see God, his was a crude variety of "disproving" God with the instruments of science. The first question for a believer is not "Can the tools of humanity demonstrate the reality of God?" but rather "Is there more than we can ever see?"

The second question uses the word "mystery" in a specific sense. One might understand the world to be a puzzle, not a mystery. A puzzle can be figured out. Our intellect may not be equal to the task, but that is not a statement about the nature of the world, but about our inadequacy. The solution exists and we just cannot get there. Mysteries, as we are using the word here, remain unsolvable; they are beyond the capacity of intellect.

———

HUMAN BEINGS GET great satisfaction out of solving puzzles. Generally we are taught to think of the world in terms of puzzles and solutions. A detective novel is satisfying because at the end the characters are assembled and what seemed a mystery is solved. Everything becomes clear.

Faith rejects the rational perfectibility of our science. We may think we've got all this figured out, but it does not add up as neatly as a detective novel. From its earliest days, religion has taught that at the heart of everything is not a puzzle but a mystery. We do not throw up our hands and simply confess ignorance. Each of us is charged to add to the collective wisdom. Slowly it dawned on me, however, that making sense of everything is not an obligation or even a possibility. So much of what goes on in the world, so much of what goes on even inside ourselves, is beyond our grasp. Acceptance of mystery is an act not of resignation but humility.

My experience reading Russell made clear that the same people who propose to understand the universe do not understand each other or indeed themselves. The ability to confess to bafflement struck me as a kind of spiritual triumph, a victory of truth over ego. In elementary school one of my favorite teachers used to quote the Talmud to us: "Teach your tongue to say 'I don't know.'"

Clearer and sweeter than Russell's sharp certainty is the example of the poet Robert Browning. Browning, whose verse is famously obscure, was once approached by a woman who asked the meaning of a particular stanza. "Madame," he answered, "when I wrote that only God and I knew what it meant. Now, only God knows."

WHAT IS REAL?

I SEARCHED FOR a way to deepen my questions. The more I understood about faith, the more it seemed to me built on searching as well as finding. The Hebrew Bible is full of warnings against idolatry but has none against atheism. False belief is dangerous, but the art of questioning is important if the questions are honest, persistent, and deep. Faith does not ask "Which medicine will cure this disease?" but "How can I use the experience of illness to help others?" It does not map the orbits of planets but does ask over and over again about the inexplicable twists of the human heart.

Asking questions of another is not only a sign of relationship, it is a means of establishing relationship. Abraham challenges God with a question: "Shall the Judge of all the earth not do justice?" (Gen. 18:25). Jesus on the cross also challenges God with a question from the Psalms: "My

God, my God, why have you forsaken me?" (Ps. 22:1, Matt. 27:46). Each draws closer to God by asking a daring, powerful question.

So long as I asked dismissive questions, faith seemed to me impossible. As life softened some edges and granted some wisdom, I began to ask out of genuine seeking, out of curiosity and not contempt. The very nature of a question opened my eyes to the possibility that what we cannot touch, what we cannot see, may indeed still be real.

———

QUESTIONS ARE INSUBSTANTIAL. You cannot see a question or touch or measure it. This is true not only of questions; our lives are built on the intangible. Right now you are reading marks on a page. They do not physically enter your brain. Yet in the interaction between the ink blots on the page and your brain, understanding is conveyed. Is the understanding tangible? What moved from the page to your brain? Can you point to it? How much of our lives take place in the elusive spaces of this world—how much is conveyed, like the artistry of the master musician, in the silence between the notes?

Ask a child to point to love. He will point to his heart, or perhaps to you, but there is no "place" for love. It is intangible.

When I learn something new, a scan may locate physiological changes in the brain, but the change is not the idea. You can map the currents in my brain when I feel a rush of emotion, but is the mapping the same as the feeling? Who really believes that the idea of justice or the meaning of morality is nothing more than a chemical change in the prefrontal cortex?

Consider the story of your life. Where you were born, where you grew up, what your home life was like, how you met the important people in your life. When someone asks you about yourself you make a careful selection from the countless facts of your life to portray a picture of yourself, to tell your story.

Now, where does that story exist? Does it have a physical existence? Although it may, in some sense, correspond to the synapses developed in the brain, does it actually have a *physical* existence? Did the story exist before you told it to someone?

We speak of things that exist "between" people. Is there indeed a "between"? If so, it exists in no physical space. The world is, so to speak, full of nonphysical entities that baffle our understanding. When the Psalmist asks, "Where is the place of God's glory?" he is wondering if we can speak of a place for that which is not physical. As we are accustomed to acknowledging what we cannot see, the idea of God seems less strange. Nonphysical things are real; they are the stuff of life. Our lives pivot on real things that are non-material: ideas, emotions, imagination, memory, relationships, intuition, suffering, joy, and faith. To believe only in what you can see seems a peculiar form of blindness.

———

COGNITIVE SCIENTIST DOUGLAS Hofstader puts it this way:

> "Do you believe in voices? How about haircuts? Are there such things? What are they? What, in the language of the physicist, is a hole—not an exotic black hole, but just a hole in a piece of cheese, for instance? Is it a physical thing? What is a symphony? Where in space and time does 'The Star-Spangled Banner' exist? Is it nothing but some ink trails on some paper in the Library of Congress? Destroy that paper and the anthem would still exist. Latin still *exists* but it is no longer a living language. The language of cavepeople in France no longer exists at all . . . One doesn't have to believe in ghosts to believe in selves that have an identity that transcends any living body."

While this is the stuff of freshman philosophy or late-night dorm room debate, it is also the battleground of neuroscience and modern thought. To speak of an idea is to speak of an intangible with tangible effects. To speak of consciousness (perhaps the hottest question in neuroscience) is to wonder how substance, mere matter, becomes aware of itself.

Not only do we live in constant company of the nonphysical, we cannot even adequately describe what *is* physical.

Bertrand Russell begins his classic book *Problems of Philosophy* by demonstrating how hard it is to decide if there is a table in the room, and to describe the table if there is. After examining its texture, color, and shape, Russell writes: "Two very difficult questions at once arise; namely, (1) Is there a real table at all? (2) If so, what sort of object can it be?"

All we know of Russell's table is what we experience, and our experience differs from that of others and is dependent on where we are standing, what part we touch, how hard we touch it, and on and on. We are the blindfolded men around the elephant, each feeling but a small part of the whole. Some are arrogant enough to believe we can whip off the blindfold and see everything. But since the blindfold is the brain, it is not possible.

As I began to appreciate how much of our world moves in the spaces we cannot see, the possibility of a nonphysical reality, a greater reality, took hold of me. If we, who are creatures with bodies moving in a physical world, are so dependent on things that cannot be seen, did I conclude too quickly that the nonphysical world, a nonphysical God, was an impossible illusion?

Honest people recognize the limitations of their own knowledge. God's perfection does not extend to God's creatures.

TWO WAYS TO SEE THE WORLD

INTUITING THE UNSEEN is a gift of perspective. Albert Einstein said there are two ways to see the world: as if everything is a miracle or as if nothing is a miracle. Living with an awareness of the miraculous re-enchants the world. From a flower to a star, it is easy to confuse knowing what a thing is made of with knowing what it is. Significance overspills the physical description; mastering botany is not the same as appreciating beauty. Acknowledging that overflow, what a flower *means* or what a human being *is*, not in chemical composition but in spiritual significance, is seeing everything as a miracle.

I joked with friends that I was going to rabbinical school "on spec." I needed to understand more about God and about myself. When I asked my brother what he thought of my going to rabbinical school, he said, "It's a phase." He knew that Russell's version of reality still lived in me: that faith was just my emptiness projected on the world; that science disproved the claims of religion; that religion caused the world's wars; that if only people would get rid of these unsupported beliefs, they would be happier and more prosperous.

I thought I had to surrender my questions, doubts, and intuitions of darkness in order to believe again. Increasingly, I learned that the great spirits of religious traditions do not solve all questions but live *in* the questions, and return to them again and again, not as a circle returns, but as an ascending spiral comes to the same place, each time at a higher level.

———

STUDYING AND TEACHING brought me to confront the reality of God in the lives of those I met. An intuition of God's presence can come to us in closeness to another whose spirit touches our own.

I cherish the memory of a remarkable teacher, filled with learning and gentleness, precious to me despite the ridiculous conditions under which we met.

I was a new rabbinical student and in my reading had come across the phrase "noch einmal." I approached Dr. Slomovic, knowing he spoke several languages, and introducing myself, asked him what "noch einmal" meant. "Once again," he answered.

Well, he was old, and probably hard of hearing. So I repeated, a little louder, "What does 'noch einmal' mean?" He said, a bit more emphatically, "Once again."

Poor man, I thought, must be difficult on him to make people repeat themselves all the time. "WHAT DOES 'NOCH EINMAL' MEAN?" I screamed. He looked at me with compassion, and placing his hand on my cheek, said, "'Noch einmal' *means* once again."

Sitting in his class, day after day, listening to him weave together stories of his life in the Eastern European home in which he grew up, listening to legends of the tradition and faith that survived the shocks of the twentieth century, was more powerful than any line of reasoning. Before me was faith as it is lived.

An argument looks different when it vibrates through a living person. Repeatedly in religious circles I came face to face with the force of faith, a faith that is not self-satisfied or closed-minded, but is a strength grounded in humility. Meeting such people reinforced the truth that faith is not an idea but a way to live, not a logical proposition but an outcome of encountering a noble soul. Russell made belief a question of logic; I was learning that it was a question of life.

Increasingly I was less concerned with what God might be than with what faith in God might make of me.

———— • ————

TWO

Where Does Religion Come From?

"We are not physical creatures having a spiritual experience. We are spiritual creatures having a physical experience."

Pierre Teilhard de Chardin

IF RELIGION IS a solution to a problem or the answer to a perplexity, then a better solution or a more sophisticated answer makes religion unnecessary. Worshipping the rising sun is futile once science has demonstrated the laws behind planetary orbits. Sacrificing a sheep to produce rain is less compelling once one has learned to seed the clouds. The sun rising or the rain falling is not a "problem" any longer because we can explain or control it without recourse to religion.

For those convinced that religion rests on a fantasy, there must be a problem or a need it is meant to address. Religion has threaded through every age and culture. Once we can identify and analyze that need, then—like seeding clouds in place of sacrificing sheep—better answers can take its place. Scholars need only figure out why human beings are captured by religious delusions. What is there in our makeup that inclines us to believe? How does religion help us to cope with life?

This chapter looks critically at the two most common explanations for religion—fear and evolutionary advantage. Both are useful in beginning to understand faith. Neither one alone captures its meaning or majesty. Religion begins in wonder, flourishes in relationship, and is realized through living with an awareness of holiness.

"I, a stranger and afraid
In a world I never made."

(A. E. Housman)

I am afraid of dying. While this hardly makes me unique, it does make me suspicious. Is my faith a longing for immortality? Has religion less to do with the existence of God than with fearing my own nonexistence?

In posing these questions I stand in a long line of both believers and doubters who wondered if death was the spur to belief. In modern times, this line of thought is most prominently associated with Sigmund Freud. Freud did not originate the explanation that religion comes from fear, but he became its premier advocate. Beginning with humanity's earliest stories, such as the ancient Sumerian epic of Gilgamesh chronicling a man's failed search for immortality, thinkers and poets have proclaimed death our greatest fear. Religion promises that death is not the end. That hope assuages our terror. Therefore, concluded Freud and his disciples, only those without the comforts of religion face the brutal fact of mortality.

Death robs us of the world, of everything we cherish. Most of us move through the day without constantly brooding on our certain death. The dread nonetheless lurks beneath the surface, ready to emerge. When I sit on an airplane, I feel no fear. I will read, eat, and sleep without worry. But if that plane hits turbulence, I will grip the seat and look around, startled and anxious. I suddenly realize that I am indeed afraid of flying, but the unease is submerged, waiting for turbulence to stir it up. Do we spend each moment in fear of death? Of course not. But when we are sick, or scared—when life hits turbulence—we feel the fear. Can this be the source of religion? Are believers at some deep level simply more frightened than those who do not believe?

The equation is elegant: fear = faith.

That equation is as reductive as every equation that shrinks a complex phenomenon to an "only": Love is *only* sex; goodness is *only* a strategy of selfish genes; people are *only* developed apes; faith is *only* an illusion born of fear; God is *only* a human projection; and the universe is *only* an accident. Such "discoveries" are announced with an assurance that finally the illusions are gone. "Only" is not actually a victory of clear-sightedness, but an enemy of the richness of life. This is not realism. It is a failure of imagination.

———

"ONLY" RESTS ON a strategy too common in religious debate. One side claims its position is based on argument and the other side is based on psychology. I am an atheist because of reason, and you are a believer because you had a bad mother, or an insufficient father, or out of terror or weakness. As a religious person I have often encountered this. "You believe in God because you need a crutch," implying, of course, that the balanced person speaking to me needs no such crutch. I know the argument because I used to believe it. I was a strong, self-confident atheist in a world of weak, credulous believers. Only they were not so weak; I was not so strong.

No single arc covers all human complexity. As much as we fear death, we value love, create meaning, hope passionately for the good of those we care for, and are disturbed by the potency of jealousy, anger, and distrust. Does religion address all of these? Yes, and so much more. Isolating one aspect of religious meaning—death or morality or community—and making it "all" about that is to make religion simple-minded.

I have known religious people all my life. Among them are unkind, small-minded, tyrannical, or even cowardly people. A few have used faith to appear selfless while prosecuting monstrously selfish agendas. Most, however, engage in innumerable activities of kindness, charity, and selflessness. They set up soup kitchens, create networks of volunteers to visit the sick, contribute money and skills to help the poor, and pray for others in need. Few of them do it because they fear death. Far stronger is the impulse to responsibility, to living a sacred life, a life of service.

Throughout my various illnesses, I prayed. My prayer was not answered because I lived; my prayer was answered because I felt better able to cope with my sickness. Each time I go for my regular tests, the CT or PET scans or an MRI, each time I am moved into the metal tube that will give an image of sickness or health, I pray. I do not pray because I believe God will give me a clear scan. I pray because I am not alone, and from gratitude that having been near death I am still in life. I pray not for magic but for closeness, not for miracles but for love.

The novelist George Meredith wrote, "Who rises from his prayer a better man, his prayer is answered." Spiritual aspiration is a likelier origin of religion than fear. Deep in us is a powerful urge to be better than we are. People of faith gaze less into the grave than up at the stars.

EXPLAINING RELIGION BY EVOLUTION

THOSE WILLING TO concede that religion is a product of more than fear are often moved to use a second strategy to account for its appeal. These days religion, and a great deal else, is explained by evolutionary psychology. The ancient environment of the savannahs of Africa and what we needed to survive there is pressed into service to explain differences in men and women, why we are attracted or repulsed by certain foods, body types, ideas, almost everything. So the craving for sweets is an adaptation to a world where fruit was a good source of sugar energy, and where chocolate chip ice cream did not exist. To our lasting regret, the craving for sweets is now maladaptive, and gorging on ice cream is more likely to result in obesity and diabetes than a rare and needed burst of energy.

———

IS RELIGION SIMILARLY maladaptive? Here is Richard Dawkins: "The religious behaviour may be a misfiring, an unfortunate by-product of an underlying psychological propensity which in other circumstances is, or once was, useful." That everything from the cathedral at Chartres to relief missions is a result of an evolutionary misfiring is impossible to maintain. When a vast phenomenon is seen through one lens, and a dismissive one at that, smart people are moved to say thoughtless things.

———

THERE ARE TWO major objections that critics have advanced to the sweeping explanations of evolutionary psychology. First is how little is known for certain about the lives of our prehistoric forebears. I once read a claim that men favor long hair because if the hair is lustrous, it proves that a woman has been healthy for a long time. It is a very plausible explanation.

Long hair may be attractive for other reasons as well. It is hard to maintain, and so suggests that the person is surrounded by others who can take care of her. Conversely, it may indicate that the person is able, and a good caretaker, since she can handle difficult-to-manage hair. Or perhaps because in the world of forests and underbrush hair is likely to get entangled, which is dangerous (think of the biblical story of Absalom, whose revolt was ended when he was captured dangling helplessly, his hair ensnared in a tree). Therefore, long hair demonstrates that the person is pampered because she can stay home and need not go out hunting or running through the bush.

The point here is not to disprove the explanation given in the article. Rather, it is to remind us that we do not live in prehistoric times and cannot know for sure what sparked certain tendencies. The Soviet dissident Miroslav Dijas said that the hard thing about being a communist was predicting the past. In Russia historical figures were always being

alternately discredited and rehabilitated. The same is true
with some of the interpretations of evolutionary psychology.
The past changes with the new interpretation of the present.
No one knows how the first ancestors of human beings created religion. Religion is in any case too various to have any
single origin.

The second challenge to evolutionary psychology is how
much of human behavior is genetic and how much is cul-
turally conditioned. Is religion built into our genes or do we
in some deep sense *choose* to be religious?

―――――

DOES EVOLUTION DETERMINE our choices? In modern
America, a preternaturally thin model of women is considered fashionable or desirable. This is clear from the anorexia
that afflicts so many models and, by societal trickle down,
so many teenage girls. Living in Los Angeles I am a daily
witness to the pressures on young women to be thinner.
The proliferation of eating disorder clinics and experts is
eloquent testimony to the prevalence of this "ideal."

Judging from movie stars and magazines, men are drawn
to thin women. Presumably this is an evolutionary predis-
position because thin, healthy women were favored in the
prehistoric savannah. Must be hard to outrun a tiger if you
are obese. Once more, the evolutionary explanation has
come to our aid.

What do we then do with models of earlier societies that favor more ample body types? Why were the women in Rubens' paintings considered so desirable when any of them would be thought too heavy today? You can answer that fat was thought to exhibit health a few hundred years ago and thinness was not, but that merely proves the point. If we were conditioned to see a certain body type as healthy for millions of evolutionary years, how could that perception change in just a century or two? Evolution is vital in explaining why we do what we do, but it is not everything. The average weight of runway models diminished in the '90s, which alone tells us that the "ideal" is changeable.

———

EVEN WHEN THE evolutionary explanation proves convincing, it remains true that the origin of something is not the explanation of it. If the proverbial apple never struck Newton in the head, gravity still exists. Even if religion came solely from fear, that says nothing as to its truth. Too often the drive to explain religion is actually the drive to explain it away.

There remains no good reason to suppose that religion is a misfired strategy of survival. Rather, it is a response to a reality beyond us. Far from being trapped in tribal illusions, we are liberated by transcendent truths.

YOUR GENES ARE SELFISH, NOT MINE

FOR YEARS THE fashionable phrase in popular biology has been "the selfish gene." Individuals may not always reproduce themselves, but genes do. That is the presumed key to human behavior. Parents will sacrifice themselves for their children because children carry parental genes. All of us, in the end, are programmed to perpetuate our own genes through those most closely related to us.

Viewed mechanically, such assumptions founder: Wealthier families, rather than having more children, have fewer children. If life was an elaborate masked ball to pass along genes, an increase in wealth should lead to an increase in offspring since wealth brings the possibility of supporting larger families. Moreover, if all we cared about was having more children, then who would ever have an abortion when adoption is possible? No one doubts that reproduction is a powerful human drive (and, incidentally, the very first commandment in the Bible) but we are not automatons. Civilization is also culture and choice.

Human beings are self-creators. Too much popular science reads as if we are our genetics and denies the possibility that we can make ourselves anew.

The resources of the human spirit continually transcend the presumed limitations of biology or conditioning. A member of my congregation, now ninety years old, was captured as a youth by the Nazis. Max trained himself to be a medic so that he would be useful in the concentration camps. As a result, although he survived the war, he was in eighteen different camps. The evil he witnessed is unimaginable. I asked him once how he survived.

"When the Nazis came for me," he said, "I told my mother that if she heard I was shot or hung, it might be true. But if they said I starved, she shouldn't believe it. There was no way I would fail to survive," he said, "so long as the there remained any chance at all to live." Each day, he managed to figure out what he needed to do to keep going. After the war he created a very successful real estate company which he still runs now into his nineties. He attends services regularly and credits God with enabling him to endure. He is not under the illusion that faith can guarantee survival. Rather, he tells me there is no way he could have survived without it. Max's fate was written not in his genes, but in his will and in his faith.

———

DESPITE THE FASHIONABLE theorizing, no single answer to the origins of religion can be adequate. Religion is neither an answer to a question nor the solution to a problem. It is a response to the wonder of existence and a guide to life. It cannot be dismissed by claiming that we "now know the answers" to the questions it has raised.

THE CAVE PAINTINGS—LOOK UP!

IN 1879, MARCELINO de Sautuola entered the cave at
Altamira accompanied by his five-year-old daughter. He was
searching for prehistoric artifacts, never suspecting that the
cave walls were a canvas for our ancient ancestors. For years
he had been studying the floor of the cave. Looking around
once more, his search was unavailing. His daughter, on her
first visit, looked up. Suddenly she called out to him, "Look
Papa, oxen!" He too looked up and there he discovered the
famous Paleolithic cave paintings.

———

THE LITTLE GIRL who looked up in the cave reminds us
of a source of faith at least as potent as fear—wonder. Religion, taught theologian A. J. Heschel, is what we do with
our wonder. We may associate the sense of wonder with
children, but its presence in our earliest years should not
blind us to its depth. Awe, amazement, and the sheer exhil-
aration of existence animate faith. "The statement 'God is'
is an understatement," Heschel declared. To feel the reality
of that truth is overwhelming.

"The world will not perish for want of wonders," said biologist J. B. S. Haldane, "but for want of wonder."

———

THE BIBLE GIVES no account of how Abraham came to recognize God; that decisive step in religious history is shrouded in silence. The ancient rabbis rush in with tales to fill the void.

One story compares Abraham to a traveler who sees a palace in flames. He cries out, "Is there no one responsible for this palace?" From an upper window the owner peeks through to assure the frightened traveler that he is responsible. The palace has an owner. Similarly, Abraham, seeing the carnage in the world, wonders if the world is uncared for. God comes to Abraham in response to his cry.

The twist to this tale is that the Hebrew for "in flames" is *doleket*. *Doleket* can also mean "full of light." So perhaps Abraham saw the world as a blazing fire or as a brilliant light, as a cauldron of injustice or as a palette of beauty. Did he think so terrible a world must have a monarch—or so magnificent a world must have a Creator?

Do we come to God from tragedy or joy, from sadness or wonder? The answer is both and more, for at the root of faith is not a solution, but a relationship.

From all that I have seen in the capacity of people to endure I know as well that tragedy and joy are often the same. My cancer brought me moments of intimacy and love I would not otherwise have known. The people who cared for me, who expressed concern, and who shared their own stories because I shared mine, all light my way. Suffering can open the soul. It can enable us to be close to others in a new way and most experiences of life carry both meanings of *doleket*; they are light and flame, both at once.

THE SECRET OF RELATIONSHIP

LOVE MODELS THE intimacy of faith. God feels suddenly real, inexplicably present, in a flash of closeness, a sudden flush of love. Questions do not disappear, instead they come before One who receives them. In relationship, answers are not solutions, but the affirmation of worth and closeness.

The theologian Martin Buber explained relationships using his coinage I-Thou. Buber taught that no one exists in isolation; there is no simple "I" by itself. We are always in relationship to others—our family, our friends, our loved ones—even if they are not present. The quality of our lives is in the quality of our ties to others.

When standing before a couple during their wedding, pronouncing the blessings, I am often struck by those gathered around them. A couple does not come under the wedding canopy alone. Parents, siblings, friends—all have combined to create the people who are pledging themselves to one another. For that moment I see a snapshot of the filaments that bind us one to the other.

Still, the bride and groom, at that moment, are most real to one another. I-Thou represents relationship at its most intense. I-Thou occurs in moments when we are fully present. For an instant I think of the other person not in terms of what I need, but rather I give fully of myself to know another. It is a complete encounter. In such flashes of intimacy there is a confluence of luck and will. That is, you must be prepared for such a moment but you cannot force it. As with all of life, the noblest spots of time are when we are prepared for marvels that await us.

Buber teaches that religion comes not out of fear, and not even out of goodness, but out of a yearning for closeness. Religion is relationship, but in this case relationship with God is the model and source of all relationship. When in the Bible, after long suffering, Job declares to God, "I heard you with my ears but now I see you with my eyes" (Job 42:5). It is the moment of awakening. This is the moment we all have, at our best. At such times we do not look to God for goods, wealth, or protection. God becomes alive to us not for what we "get" but for the inexpressible joy of closeness. When I tell the couple that they stand together with God, each feels the power of that union.

―――――

RELIGION IS A phenomenon of community, but also of the individual seeking soul in relationship to God. The peak moment of the Hebrew Bible makes this clear by recounting that the Ten Commandments were delivered to a people, but they are addressed in the singular. We are many but we are one. I sat with many other campers in that movie almost forty years ago, but it was still my heart that broke. I stood with other students on a peak called "Arthur's Seat" in Edinburgh in college, having climbed together, but it was my heart that felt uplifted by the possibility that I stood in God's presence. I stand by the bedside of a colleague, another rabbi with cancer, and we are together but each of us holds unspeakable secrets in our own hearts. Relationship ties us to one another, to be sure, but we each stand before the universe in our individual uniqueness. For each soul God waits.

———

LIVED RELIGION IS far more encompassing than any single explanation of religion's origins. Praying with one who is ill is religion, but so is singing hymns with a congregation and studying sacred scripture and celebrating holidays and expressing silent thanks in moments of joy and doing relief work in the wake of a disaster and a thousand other tasks or observances. One can have simple faith, but faith is not simple.

THE QUESTION REVISITED

THE SEARCHING THAT began in my teens has never ended. Although a practicing rabbi, the same questions drive me now that drove me then—they are the questions that drive this book. But for me a picture has emerged and it is tied together by two questions and two answers.

The questions are simple in themselves: Why are we here, and why is anything here?

In certain moments, the marvel of the fact that we exist strikes the receptive soul. Here we return to Einstein's comment about seeing everything as a miracle, or nothing as a miracle. If we are awestruck by existence, then everything in it, cruel and kind, will have a sheen of the miraculous. It does not make it all desirable or good, but surely it remains miraculous. For as philosopher Gottfried Leibniz asked several hundred years ago, why is there anything rather than nothing, when nothing is so much easier than something?

We are not accidental. Through questioning, living, suffering, comforting, lamenting, and loving, I now understand that my life is in response. There is a call; for me that call grew more poignant when the doctor told me my test indicated lymphoma. Strange though it may sound, I heard God's whisper through the sadness: You do not have forever. Whatever you are charged to do in this world must be done. It was on that day, though I did not yet know it, that I began this book.

————

THE CALL IS in the very fact of existence. For a long time I looked only inward, but at last, like the child in the cave, I looked up.

In my life, moments of miracle are not only in extraordinary moments. The birth of my daughter was such a moment. Yet walking down a street can be a moment of miracle. Standing before God is not a condition of the world but of the soul. I can feel it in the most unlikely times. Giddy and grateful for existence, I feel my heart grow. Not for a moment do I believe that this everyday ecstasy begins in me. It is there always, always to be felt, to move through us. We receive God and give God forth; we are both cisterns and fountains.

Moments of pain can also be moments of miracle: times of urgency, when the world needs our voice and our hands. Even our silence can be in answer to a call. From time to time I realize, speaking to someone in trouble or in pain, that if I can only be quiet, only return the person to himself, that healing can occur. I once sat with a child whose illness tested both him and his family. His parents tried every answer to make it "right," to explain it, to justify what had happened. I sat with him in my office for almost fifteen minutes in absolute silence. The air felt charged with meaning that I did not entirely understand, so I waited for him to speak. Suddenly, without warning, he cried. From that instant he and his family began to learn how to live with his condition.

———

I'VE OFTEN TOLD children the story of a man who stood before God, his heart breaking from the pain and injustice in the world. "Dear God," he cried out, "Look at all the suffering, the anguish and distress in Your world. Why don't you send help?"

God responded: "I did send help. I sent you."

To respond is to feel one has been sent. The Bible depicts prophets who are sent despite their own wishes. Moses is coerced, Jeremiah is compelled, Samuel does not even understand at first that it is God's voice he hears, and must be called repeatedly before recognizing it. Religion is not a fantasy projected upward but a call received.

We are enjoined, in the Biblical image, to tend the garden. Improving the world is the mission to which faith has always pledged its efforts, however badly it has failed at times. When I walk in the halls of my synagogue and see volunteers stuffing envelopes inviting the community to a charitable event, that is religion too. Religion happens in committee rooms as well as homeless shelters. The essential task of religion in this world is to heal, to help, to repair what has been shattered. It is therefore a strange and painful irony that religion has often made the world worse, not better, and broken lives instead of mending them.

The quality of religion's response does not prove if it is true, but it does prove if it is worthy. Religion as an answer to God can only be valuable if the answer is one that elevates the human spirit.

Religion's record in history is mixed. No believer can fail to be shamed by the cruelties practiced in the name of God.

Still, the historical record is better than some of its detractors claim. Those who respond to God's call are not angels, but human beings. Their efforts will be marred by human failings. The reputation of religion will suffer terribly from those who too often speak in its name.

We do expect a great deal from religion, as we should. When I speak to the staff of the synagogue, I remind them that each one of us, from groundskeepers to teachers to maintenance people to clergy, represent the institution and by extension, faith itself. Phone calls of complaint always begin the same way: the caller asks, "How is it possible that in a SYNAGOGUE . . . ?" The clear message is: "We expect more from a religious institution. I might be treated this way in a business office, but a house of God should do better."

Is it religion itself, or religion that betrays its own highest ideals, that causes divisiveness and conflict? In all the charges made about religion, particularly in our own day, none is more common and more virulent than the charge that religion is what causes conflict, hate, and war. An honest look at human nature and at the historical record teaches that religion has much more good to claim than is usually acknowledged.

———— •◆• ————

THREE

Does Religion Cause Violence?

They say "peace, peace," but there is no peace.
Jeremiah 6:14

THE BUS TO THE END OF THE WORLD

ONE SUMMER WHILE backpacking through Israel I spent two hours at the site of the world's end. Armageddon, in Hebrew called "Megiddo," is where the New Testament's Book of Revelation teaches the ultimate battle is to take place preceding the Messianic age. It is a quiet little hill, a good place to reflect upon the question of violence in religion.

Buses don't often run past Megiddo. If you have to trans-
fer you should hope for the kind of bright sky and soft wind
that prevailed that day as I waited, standing beside an old
lady carrying a shopping bag. The fevered dreams of apocalyptic war seemed far away as we both sat and stood, shifting our weight, waiting for the next bus. Looking at her bag
I remembered the poem "Tourists" by Israeli poet Yehuda
Amichai; Amichai describes sitting with two baskets under
a Roman arch in Jerusalem. A tour guide points out the arch
to his group by noting it is just above the head of the man
with shopping baskets. And the poet thinks that redemption would arrive if only the tour guide would say, "You see
that arch from the Roman period? It's not important: but
next to it, left and down a bit, there sits a man who's bought
fruit and vegetables for his family."

Amichai's poem points out how easy it is to favor history
and grand stories over everyday life. People grow more attached to symbols, at times, than they do to human beings.
The story of religious violence is in part a story of losing the
person behind the symbol.

Religious violence is real but it is a small part of the lives
of most believers. More powerful by far is the guidance religion offers to live decently and to care for others. There are
many more people carrying shopping baskets than sharpen-
ing their swords for the final battle.

Nonetheless there *is* a long history of conflict in religion.
While faith has been filled with fighting, fighting, however,

is not ultimately caused by faith. From soccer stadiums to schoolyards, we see that human beings are passionate, easily angered, and filled with both kindness and rage. The trigger of violence is found less in sacred books than in human nature.

Cain and Abel were the first recorded siblings. One murdered the other. The Bible tells us from the outset that we must not imagine that the human story will be one of uninterrupted peace.

In my work I am daily witness to families torn apart by jealousies, by rivalries, by insults real and imagined, by money. These fights are not caused by religion, though religion can at times moderate the parties and remind them of something higher than self-interest. I recently asked a brother who was denying his sister a share of their parent's inheritance, "Would God want you to do this?" The question meant, "Will you place family and faith above material goods?" He struggled with the question and relented. They shared the inheritance because the conflict was not caused by faith, but could be cured by it.

What is true on a small scale can be true for history and politics. Religion can encourage the separatist tendencies in our nature and appeal to our sense of exclusivity. When we look at history, however, we find that without faith the world has grown closer to darkness and despair.

THE CHALLENGE OF OUR TIME

HOSTILITY TOWARD RELIGION was greatly exacerbated the day that terrorists flew hijacked planes into the Twin Towers. An event combining technology, politics, religion, and culture did not swell calls for an end to technology or politics, only religion. Religion was implicated because of a long record of inciting people against one another, spurring them to resentment and fostering violence. The terrorists who carried out the attack were quite clear that they did so in the name of Islam. There were cries that have echoes today of people fed up with religion, pointing to the protracted trail of religious conflict: the Sunni and Shia battle; the long history of war between Protestants and Catholics; Buddhist and Sikh violences, schisms inside the Jewish and Hindu communities as well as their record of being parties to other conflicts.

Religion is not our enemy. Before the Western faiths captured the heart of our world there was cruelty, carnage, and destruction. In the twentieth century, when religion ceased to be a force in international politics, the scale of slaughter was far beyond anything human beings had ever known. Religion's place in conflict cannot be understood if we compare it to a perfect, peaceful world, such as we have never seen. The question is rather, "What sort of world did religion come into, and what did it make of that world? What is the world like when we take religion out of it?" Only by comparing the ages when religion was dominant with the ages when it was weak or absent can we fairly estimate the depredations or benefactions of faith.

THE HISTORIAN AND THE PHILOSOPHER

EDWARD GIBBON WAS a contemplative individual, a man of the enlightenment, not a believer in any sort of God. In 1764, sitting amidst the ruins of the Capitol in Rome, he first conceived his life's work. His long, rolling sentences express an erudition and historical insight that together created the greatest single work of history in the English language: *The History of the Decline and Fall of the Roman Empire.*

One safe generalization about empires up to the present day is that they fall. All ancient empires fell: Assyria, Babylonia, Persia, the Mongols. Modern empires are either gone or severely diminished: the Ottomans, the Dutch, the British, and the Soviet. Among all these empires, the question of why Rome fell excites the greatest interest. Each year books are produced with new theories or elaborations on why Rome fell. Theories range from the likely to the implausible, from imperial overstretch (i.e., trying to conquer far-flung territories) to lead poisoning to economic troubles to corruption. No single cause can account for such a great historical event. Yet Gibbon thought he hit upon the major reason for Rome's fall: Christianity.

His picture of Christianity is caustic. Gibbon parades before us corrupt officials, misguided saints, and hypocritical professions of faith. None of these, however, is the cause of Rome's fall in Gibbon's view. On the contrary—Rome fell not because of the betrayal of Christian ideals, but because of their fulfillment. Christianity was too pacifistic, thought Gibbon, stripping the great empire of its fighting brio. Christian teachings of meekness and kindness took away the martial pride of the Roman soldier. In other words, it was not sufficiently warlike:

> The clergy successfully preached the doctrines of patience and pusillanimity; the active virtues were discouraged; and the last remains of the military spirit were buried in the cloister; a large portion of public and private wealth as consecrated to the specious demands of charity and devotion; and the soldiers' pay was lavished on the useless multitudes of both sexes, who could only plead the merits of abstinence and chastity.

In time the Roman empire became the Christian empire. Christianity developed as a world religion and matters of state became intertwined with theology. Despite Gibbon's fears that Christianity was too peaceful, militarism did not disappear. The Holy Roman Empire still fought and killed. The militarism that was an inheritance from Rome was moderated, although hardly eliminated. What changed was the drive toward peace. For the great religions teach that peace is God's desire and humanity's obligation, not as a result of conquest but because of Divine mandate.

Gibbon's is not the only testimony of Christianity's docility. Gibbon argued that Christianity's peaceful nature ruined the ancient world of Rome. Later and even more important thinkers argued that Judaism and Christianity's values of nonviolence were ruining the modern world of Europe.

Friedrich Nietzsche was a German philosopher and classicist who fashioned modern notions of power. Though Nietzsche is an enormously controversial figure, no one doubts his acuity in diagnosing the pains of modernity. Nietzsche wrote short, sharp aphorisms and Gibbon long, Latinate paragraphs, but they shared a fundamental disapproval of Christian ideals. Here is Nietzsche on the morality of Judaism and Christianity:

> All that has been done on earth against "the noble" "the powerful," "the masters," "the rulers," fades into nothing compared with what the *Jews* have done against them . . . It was the Jews who with awe-inspiring consistency, dared to invert the aristocratic value-equation (good = noble = powerful = beautiful = happy = beloved of God) and to hang on to this inversion with their teeth . . . saying "the wretched

alone are the good; the poor, impotent, lowly alone
are the good; the suffering, deprived, sick, ugly alone
are pious, alone are blessed by God, blessedness is for
them alone—and you, the powerful and noble, are on
the contrary the evil, the cruel, the lustful, the insa-
tiable, the godless to all eternity; and you shall be in
all eternity the unblessed, accursed, and damned!" . . .
One knows *who* inherited this Jewish revaluation . . .
with the Jews there begins *the slave revolt in morality*:
that revolt which has a history of two thousand years
behind it and which we no longer see because it—has
been victorious.

Nietzsche teaches that there are two forms of morality, the master morality and the slave morality. The Greek
legacy, the morality of the master, is that the beautiful and
powerful and potent are beloved of the gods. Along come
the Jews, who are powerless and cannot remedy their situa-
tion in the usual way, by making war. So they take spiritual
revenge on their oppressors: They claim that the oppressed
are loved by God. The bereaved and bereft are loved by
God. Christianity spread this ethic throughout the world.
In his writings, Nietzsche tirelessly inveighs against the
ethic of "pity, self-denial and self-sacrifice."

Nietzsche and Gibbon were classicists, scholars of the
ancient world. Classicists "know" from the history of antiquity that the natural state of things is war. The soldier, the

military hero, was the one to be revered. Ancient heroes like Achilles or Odysseus are not seen as heroic for their morality but their cunning and military prowess. To propose an ideal of peace based on love and fraternity rather than strength was scandalous, contrary to human nature, and would never work.

Writings attacking religion frequently quote both Gibbon and Nietzsche. What they omit is their central concern about Christianity, that it idealizes peace. Mildness overthrew Rome; morality is a way of disarming force in the name of moral suasion. Meekness, the slave morality that believes the oppressed is to be beloved, is a legacy of Judaism and then Christianity that aroused in Nietzsche the kind of contempt that makes him an ally of those who revile modern faith.

Why does no one today talk about Christianity as failing because it is too peaceful? The history of religious violence, East and West, would make such an argument impossible. I do not seek to prove that religious history is a chronicle of peace. No one would be so blind or so foolish. There is a serious case to be made, however, that religion is *not* the primary cause for war, and that a world without religion is liable to be as violent, or more violent, than a world with faith.

Every generation enters the world *in medias res*—in the middle of the story. Only history can explain the story in which we find ourselves. Religion is bound up with a great deal of conflict, but to know how crucial the religious element is we must know what came before. What did come before monotheism—was it a world of peace and concord? The corollary of "war is caused by religion" should be "peace is the result of the absence of religion." It has never been that simple.

THE ANCIENT PAST:
A WORLD WITHOUT RELIGION

MONOTHEISM ENTERED THE world a little over 3,000 years ago. The study of prehistory teaches us that before monotheism the world was anything but peaceful. Living before humanity recognized one God was hardly living in Eden. In fact, warfare was more common in antiquity than it is in modern society; one scholar estimates that 65 percent of ancient tribal societies were at war continuously. The world of 10,000 BCE was a world of astonishing aggression.

When the fog of pre-history lifts, civilization is still scarred by war.

THE CLASSICAL WORLD

GREECE AND ROME together are the apogee of the classical world. They have also left us a legacy of appalling violence. During the fifth century BCE the Peloponnesian war pitted the city-states of Athens and Sparta and their allies against each other in a long contest for dominance. The island of Melos pleaded neutrality. When threatened by Athens, the citizens of Melos insisted they wished to be an enemy of neither Athens nor Sparta. Athens then proclaimed the kind of ideal that would warm Nietzsche's heart: "The strong do what they can and the weak suffer what they must." The Melians did not relent and as a result, every man of military age was put to the sword, and all the women and children sold into slavery.

Students of ancient Rome study Caesar's genocidal campaigns, the obliteration of Carthage, and the seemingly endless civil war. The slaughter was not in the name of any religious faith. Rome followed in the bloodthirsty traditions of preceding powers: the Persian Empire, the Babylonian Empire, the Assyrian Empire. The Western world—for that is the world we are focusing on in this summary—before Christianity was a chronicle of cruelty, punctuated by the flowering of individual genius and scattered devotion to goodness.

Rome and Greece bequeathed great riches to the world— law and philosophy, poetry, art, and architecture—all the beneficences of the classical age. Throughout antiquity genius flourished, but against a backdrop of great mercilessness. From the pre-classical Assyrian conquests to Alexander the Great's razing of Thebes, life was, as the philosopher

Thomas Hobbes memorably wrote, "solitary, poor, nasty, brutish and short." The decline of the classical world was a tragedy in many ways, but the tragedy was the result not of the rise of Christianity but of the barbarian invasions. Those invasions destroyed the culture that later medieval monks, in the East and West, managed partially to preserve. The invasions were not a result of religion. Rather, they were the legacy of tribes untouched by the idea of one God. The world was ruled by the kind of people who "wade through slaughter to a throne/ And shut the gates of mercy on mankind."

———

THE POINT OF this brief tour is to remind ourselves that religion did not bring fighting into the world. Religion entered a world in which human beings fought, over and over again. The antidote to the simple conclusion that religion causes war is to remind ourselves that people have always fought because, alas, that is what people do. Conquest and subjection are part of the dispiriting narrative of human history at all times, in all parts of the world. In the succinct and often quoted words of the ancient historian Tacitus, explaining how conflicts were resolved in his world: "They make a desolation and call it 'peace.'"

THE CRUSADES AND THE INQUISITION

THE "AGE OF faith" is what historians often call the time following Rome and Greece. Now Christianity had conquered much of the western world. Once monotheism, the conviction of the reality of One God, entered the world, bloodshed and warfare did not end. There was no sudden outbreak of universal peace. The Crusades and the Inquisition alone remind us that religion is capable of great evil. Is there any difference between the world before monotheism and the world directly after?

Rarely have I entered a debate about religion without hearing, "What about the Crusades and the Inquisition?" Fair enough. Christian rule has a great deal to answer for. As a Jew, I am keenly aware that the cruelties of Christianity (and Islam) over the centuries have caused my ancestors tremendous suffering. Both the Crusades and the Inquisition are notable for the pain inflicted on Jews who were largely powerless.

However, neither the Crusades nor the Inquisition were solely religious events. There was a powerful struggle between church and state in the High Middle Ages. Behind the lofty phrases was a great deal of what we call today realpolitik.

In all these battles, religious zeal played a large role, but religion is virtually always allied with politics and power when it explodes into violence. The Crusades were not born in a vacuum. The Crusades were a prolonged call for soldiers from Christendom to retake Jerusalem from Islam. The Latin West retained the memory of lands that had been theirs between 300 BCE and 600 CE. Along the way, debts were cancelled, reputations made or restored, kingdoms won and lost. Land, treasure, and power intertwined in this as in all great historical conflicts. Rarely, if ever, is it just about religion.

To the extent that the Crusades were a purely religious persecution unrelated to land and power, they were directed against the Jews. There are chronicles of Jews who survived, telling of the slaughter in towns all along the Crusaders' route to Jerusalem. Christian anti-Semitism has caused untold suffering, and today Moslem anti-Semitism is an ominous development. Hatred is hardly restricted to those who are believers, but there is no whitewashing the horrific effects that such religious hatred can have and have had throughout history. Religion teaches the kinship of all human beings, which should tie us together, but alongside such teachings is an often frighteningly exclusive idea of the path to God. Parochial paths to God can license the believer to be cruel to those who oppose or disagree. The Crusades killed many out of just such a conviction. This mercilessness reminds us of the internal battle that religions need to fight—the tendency to make God as narrow as we can be ourselves.

———

TWO CENTURIES AFTER the Crusades came the Inquisition, a long and bitter blight on Christian history. The Inquisition was a long quasi-legal attempt to root out heresy in the church. Converted Jews, new Christians, were particular targets because the inquisitors suspected them of insincerity and of corrupting the Christian population. Although, according to the most recent research, fewer than 10,000 people were executed in the 300 years of the Inquisition—a number far smaller than we might expect—each death was a triumph of intolerance. The Inquisition, also responsible for countless exiles and broken lives, was particularly frightening in its attempt to control thought. Inquisitors tortured people and paid informers to discover the "true" beliefs of those acting as Christians. The fettering of free thought can prove in the end to be even more dangerous than physical coercion.

Complications do arise, however, just when we think we have history pinned down. The Inquisition was actually at its most lenient in the Vatican-controlled lands in Italy. Spain and Portugal expelled Jews at the end of the fifteenth century, but the Vatican allowed them to reside in the papal State. Within religions, even at their most extreme times, there are those who offer a gentler reading of God's will.

Once again we find political considerations involved, since the identification of an enemy population served Spanish monarchs Ferdinand and Isabella as a means to unite their realm. Religion proved a convenient tool for rulers to identify the "others" and persecute them.

The Inquisition and Crusades are painful even beyond the suffering they inflicted. For they were a betrayal of the ideals of the faiths in whose names they were fought. Evil in the name of God is particularly vile. Again and again in history, presumed believers denigrated teachings of peace in favor of those that countenanced brutality.

———

THE RELIGIOUS WARS of Europe ended in the 1648 peace of Westphalia. These wars had national components as well (German princes rebelling against the Habsburg Empire, for example) but they were wars largely impelled by religious animosities. Westphalia marked a slowly maturing process in the western world: the separation of church and state. The strategy of not imposing religion on one's citizens was in the long run healthy both for religion and for state. Forcing temporal governments to instantiate eternal ideals was neither good for the governments nor for the ideals. The seeds of this realization were long in sprouting in the minds of human beings, but they did grow.

The majority of conflicts in human history have controlling motivations that are not religious. Despite the promises of faith, most people are more likely to risk fighting for rewards in this world than promises of the next. And there is a tension in wars of religion between ideals and violence. We may be sure that no one in ancient Assyria stood up and cried, "How can we fight like this? It is cruel! After all, we are Assyrians!" Assyrians fought untroubled by conscience. Romans cheered the brutalities of the arena. But love for peace runs through all the major religions. Three hundred years before the Athenians slaughtered the people of Melos, Isaiah declared, "Nation shall not lift up sword against nation, neither shall they learn war any more" (Is. 2:4). The impulse to peace exists in religion, and in times of violence believers of goodwill can seek out that impulse and help it grow.

THE DAWN OF THE MODERN AGE

FOR OVER A century (1337–1453) France and Britain fought their "Hundred Years' War." A standard college textbook reads: "The causes of the conflicts known as the Hundred Years' War were thus dynastic, feudal, political, and economic." Religion is not even mentioned. One who assumes that Western history is all about religious war will find this omission shocking. It prepares us, however, for a world in which religion is no longer the powerful force it was in earlier days. What will happen when governments cease to be controlled by religious faith? Will the world grow peaceful? We can look at the past few centuries for the answer: This is a world in which war grew more fierce, not less.

The "Second Hundred Years' War" in the eighteenth century was far more destructive than its namesake, its toll on human life far greater. Figures are hard to come by, but estimates of casualties across Europe reach five million. To retain perspective, consider that the total population of England in the 1750s was about six million. This power-driven conflagration became what historian David Bell calls "The First Total War."

Once the sovereignty of religion began to break down, the pace of slaughter grew exponentially. Military technology went hand in hand with a cheapening of human life.

Throughout the eighteenth century it became possible for states to make decisions largely freed from religious considerations. The long struggle for power between religious and secular authorities was decisively won by the state.

Did the absence of church from state promote possibilities for peace? Looking at French society a mere four years after the Revolution, which swept away clerical power, offers an answer. In 1793, the "people's revolution" was, as historian Michael Burleigh writes, "the first occasion in history when an 'anticlerical' and self-styled 'non-religious' state embarked on a program of mass murder that anticipated many twentieth-century horrors." A quarter of a million people were killed.

Listen to the words of the French revolution's "committee of public safety" in 1794: "Comrades, we enter the insurgent region. I order you to burn down everything that can be burned and to spear with your bayonets all the inhabitants you encounter along the way. I know there may be a few patriots in this region—it matters not, we must sacrifice all." From the destroyed island of Melos to the French Revolution, the voice of despotic power speaks the same language.

As poet and historical novelist Adam Thorpe writes:

"Enlightenment thought, conceiving a society built on reason and justice, saw war as barbaric and exceptional: it dreamed of perpetual peace. In the early heady months of the French revolution, this fantastical ideal seemed possible. Robespierre, in a speech to the National Assembly in May 1790, saw 'fraternity' as natural and France as the leading exponent of pacifism. Yet, within two years, his country had triggered one of the longest military bloodbaths in history."

The subsequent war, the first "total war" mentioned above (in which not only the professional military class fought, but citizens were recruited in large numbers), claimed several million lives and was fought all across Europe. No one thought it a religious war.

———

THE FRENCH REVOLUTION began in declarations of peace and ended in murder. In time, the guillotine proved insufficiently effective and mass drownings accomplished what the guillotine could not. What soon followed in this newly secularized world were the Napoleonic wars, sweeping across Europe.

The Napoleonic wars ended at Waterloo, but the hope that war would end proved elusive as ever. Half a century later the greatest conflict that ever engulfed the United States was fought, the Civil War. Here too there were believers of all kinds on both sides of the war. While the great abolitionists, from Wilberforce in England to John Brown in America, were indeed men of faith, believing that they were fulfilling the promise of scripture in freeing the slaves, there were those on the side of subjugation who claimed as well to be following the dictates of the Bible. But it was not a religious war, although both North and South were quick to claim God and the Bible in support of their aims. The greatest figure to emerge from that conflict, and perhaps the greatest in American history, was a believer, albeit no kind of conventional Christian. Abraham Lincoln spoke simply, stirringly about God with the humility that characterizes reflective faith.

The Enlightenment grew up hand in hand with the liberation of states from religious domination. The Enlightenment brought blessings of free inquiry, the greatly increased pace of scientific discovery, and unprecedented explorations of human nature. Ideas of tolerance and individuality, though they exist in religious traditions, were given shape and heft by Enlightenment thinkers. The name "Enlightenment," however, with its connotations of radiance, can be misleading. There are serious shortcomings to a philosophy of life resting on human reason alone.

Too many Enlightenment thinkers believed that human beings would be liberated from religious dogmatism to be good and do good. All humanity required was a commitment to its own liberation and devotion to reason. Instead, many of the worst instincts in human beings were liberated and there was no restraining hand of faith in a higher order.

THE TWENTIETH CENTURY AND HISTORICAL SHAME

THE TWENTIETH CENTURY was by far the bloodiest in human history. The scale of suffering is so immense that it dwarfs any power of comprehension. How much of this is the responsibility of religion is a crucial question in our world, when the convictions of the religious are so intertwined with the fate of nations.

The French Revolution and the Enlightenment opened a space that never existed before. People created new belief systems to fill the gap opened by the absence of religious systems. Alternative philosophies flourished. Humanity leapt backward from the rocky age of Faith to the genocidal age of ideology.

———

"THE GREAT WAR," "The War to End all Wars"— these were the names given to the First World War. Ironically, shortly before the outbreak of that epochal conflict, a number of books like Norman Angell's best-selling *The Great Illusion* argued that war had become too costly and awful to ever be countenanced again. A growing group of writers, politicians, and thinkers agreed that the slaughters that scarred human history were at an end.

A well-attuned ear might have caught the accents of the Enlightenment in such claims. As before, sunny predictions proved worse than merely mistaken.

In 1914 a war broke out that claimed over eight million lives. The subsequent borders drawn by the victorious powers contributed to the horrors to come, creating a patchwork world that still bedevils those who seek peace.

This was not a religious war. Its mainsprings were aristocratic Prussian militarism, the failure of diplomacy, the peculiarities and tensions in the empire systems of the world, and inadequate leadership on all sides. The improved technology of warfare combined with the momentum to create an unprecedented slaughter. This epochal tragedy was a secular and politically motivated one.

The end of the war left a world already incubating the seeds of a far greater conflict. For thousands of years the monotheistic traditions had taught that human beings were at best imperfect. No system, no social arrangement could eliminate the shadow side of the human spirit. The utopian impulse, however, the certainty that some organization of society would yield paradise, still lived inside those who had left the world of faith. Many who had been part of religions, which prayed for a messianic age with the help of God, now believed that through Communism or Nazism or Fascism, human beings could create such an age. Forcing others to be part of the envisioned "perfect" world led to unprecedented misery.

What remains when you drain transcendence from a society and leave it with the worship of human beings? You get the Nietzschean idea, the disfiguring fantasy of the ubermensch, the individual who is greater than all rules and restraints. Here is Hitler on Christianity: "The heaviest blow that was ever struck humanity was the coming of Christianity. . . ." The novelist Joseph Roth, drinking himself to death in Paris before the war, said that Hitler probably had the Christians in his sights, too. If you wish to capture the devotion of men's souls, it is best to wipe out their consciences first. This is what Nazis set out to do, at times counting on the passivity or even acquiescence of Christians throughout Europe. Individuals in whom the religious light continued to flicker, such as Dietrich Bonhoeffer, were not swept into the prevailing barbarism, and paid for their protests with their lives. Interred in concentration camps, Edith Stein, Rabbi Leo Baeck, and countless, nameless others held fast to a faith that gave them courage in the face of monstrous cruelty. Around them, God was absent from the ideology of the society and the world burned.

Did Christian anti-Semitism make it more possible for Hitler to do what he did? Without doubt. But he did not incite mass murder as a Christian. The long history of Christian contempt for Jews never created a regime like Nazism, and for good reason: The ultimate theological aim for classical Christianity was that Jews become Christians, not that Christians slaughter them. While this at times led to horrific mistreatment of Jews, genocide awaited a regime that rejected the Christian message.

What Germany would become without Christianity was understood and predicted by the great German-Jewish poet Heinrich Heine, 100 years before it came to pass, in 1834: "Christianity, and this is its greatest merit, has occasionally calmed the brutal German lust for battle, but it cannot destroy that savage joy. And when once that restraining talisman, the cross, is broken, then the old combatants will rage with the fury celebrated by the Norse poets."

———

THE YOUNG STUDENT of the future, reading the history of the twentieth century, will surely believe, as he turns the page, that he has seen the worst. No group, ideology, or government could possibly kill people with the blinkered ferocity of the Nazis. That student will then learn with sickened surprise of the toll Communism took on the twentieth century.

The Black Book is one of the painful, essential relics of the communist era. Edited by Stephane Curtois and involving an international team of scholars, it estimates the number of people killed by Communist regimes in the twentieth century. Such estimates can never reach the precision that the memory of each individual victim deserves, but for now they are the best we have to go on. The following staggering numbers of those killed are the result of societies, in each and every case, where religion was alternately persecuted, outlawed, or widely reviled:

20 million in the Soviet Union

65 million in the People's Republic of China

1 million in Vietnam

2 million in North Korea

2 million in Cambodia

1 million in the Communist states of Eastern Europe

150,000 in Latin America

1.7 million in Africa

1.5 million in Afghanistan

10,000 deaths "resulting from actions of the international communist movement and communist parties not in power"

These are not people who died in war. The statistics do not include the battles of Stalingrad or Moscow. These are the result of deportations, forced famines, and executions. This is murder, murder in the name of an ideology that denied God and expelled faith.

———

COMMUNISM'S TOLL IS unimaginable. The murders, the blighted lives, the stunting of human freedom and progress were on a wider scale than the world has seen before. While it was not the repression of faith itself that caused the terror, but rather the triumph of a pernicious ideology, would such an ideology have been able to take hold in the presence of a vigorous faith? Can it be a simple coincidence that every Communist society actively, consistently, and violently repressed religion? Every house of worship Stalin emptied and burned was an obstacle removed on the path to repression.

The Soviet Union endorsed a pseudoscience, the science of Trofim Lysenko, who punished all dissent from his mistaken theories about inheritance of acquired characteristics. Ideology shaped science in the Soviet Union while the Western world practiced real science. The free faith of the Western world made science possible. Reason and faith are not enemies. Repress faith and reason too goes out the window.

The lack of religion did not liberate the Communist world. It rather enabled what the writer Vladimir Nabokov so memorably characterized as a society of "poker faced bullies and smiling slaves."

The great tyrannies of the twentieth century were tyrannies of atheistic regimes: Mao's China, Stalin's Russia, and Hitler's Germany. Pol Pot's massacres in Cambodia were similarly done in the name of Marxist "liberation." When God is displaced from society, does the human ego expand proportionately to fill the absence? Nature, even human nature, abhors a vacuum; when our need for meaning is wrenched from its religious roots, people repeatedly turn to creeds that draw devotees by the power of their conviction. Too often adherents are moved to cruelty in the name of good or are left with a sense of emptiness. One of the wisest observers of the human condition in our time, the Holocaust survivor and psychiatrist Viktor Frankl, author of the classic *Man's Search for Meaning*, writes:

> "The gas chambers of Auschwitz were the ultimate consequence of a theory that man is nothing but the product of heredity and environment—or as the Nazis liked to say, 'of blood and soil.' I am absolutely convinced that the gas chambers of Auschwitz, Treblinka, and Maidanek were ultimately prepared not in some ministry or other in Berlin, but rather at the desks and in lecture halls of nihilistic scientists and philosophers."

———

IN HIS BOOK *God Is Not Great*, Christopher Hitchens compares North Korea to what it must be like to live with an all-present, all-knowing God. In North Korea, portraits of the "great leader" are everywhere, everyone is watched, and there is no escape.

The irony is that those who escape North Korea go to South Korea, a thriving, modern state. South Korea is also home to a vigorous Christian movement. Religion flourishes in South Korea. North Korea, however, is officially atheistic.

So the atheistic state is a totalitarian nightmare, and the state with a strong religious community is free.

DOES RELIGION CAUSE THE CONFLICT?

WHAT CAUSES HUMAN beings to fight?

Has there ever been a society without war? The answer seems to be no. Even if it were true that somewhere, in a little-known region of the world, there was a group of human beings who did not pillage, rape, and murder one another, we would still be left with the painful question: Why is this the exception?

Unfortunately for the self-image of our species, scholars now believe that in pre-state and pre-agricultural societies, male mortality from violence was about 25 percent. In other words, a quarter of all men suffered violent death, which is equal only to the most violent conflicts in subsequent history. If human always fought, then the question is not why religious societies at times go to war. It is in our nature to do so. The question is whether religion can help dampen the warring impulse.

Not only are human beings from their earliest recorded history prone to violence, but some anthropologists argue that the disappearance of the Neanderthals is attributable to early warfare. As historian Ronald Wright points out, "if it turns out that the Neanderthals disappeared because they were an evolutionary dead end, we can merely shrug and blame natural selection for their fate. But if they were in fact a variant or race of modern man, then we must admit to ourselves that their death may have been the first genocide." Human history from our first steps was plagued by the aggression in our nature.

Human interactions, from boardrooms to playgrounds, demonstrate hostility alongside cooperation. On the swings and the climbing bars, children show all the passions and impulses that later cause society heartache. When a new child comes to the park, exclusion is a foretaste of more hurtful examples. Religion at times encourages these negative traits in human beings, but it does not create them.

In the many years I have taught children in all sorts of settings, what strikes me is the enormous efforts and time society gives to civilizing human impulses. Most of what we learn of morality comes through teaching. Impulses to be unkind are instinctual. Religious tradition and simple parental guidance exist to counteract that instinct. We are born wanting for ourselves and must learn to want for others. We are born with the capacity for frustration and anger and must learn the tendency toward tolerance and gentleness. In time we can cultivate those whispering parts of ourselves, the moral instincts we were born with that tend to others, hurt for them, and reach out to help.

There may be gender distinctions here as well; classical religions often focus on the drives of men more than women, because they believe that the aggressive, angry, and destructive impulses are more alive in men. The Bible writes that at the outset of the human journey "it is not good for a man to be alone" (Gen. 2:18). Commentators note that it does not actually say "for man" but rather "for a man." Perhaps it points to the societal havoc wreaked by single men without the restraining hands of women. Still, every human being, male or female, rich or poor, of every race and every faith, has a powerful disposition to do that which can harm others.

Religion's potential for cruelty is unsurprising since we bring that cruelty with us. Religion seeks to restrain it, although by a kind of ideological jujitsu, it sometimes contributes to the very violence it seeks to tame.

How do we stand in nature? Here is a remarkable passage with a sting in its tail, from *Island Sojourn* by Elizabeth Arthur:

"There are two kinds of animals in this world, the killers and the runners. They can be distinguished by the shape of their jaws and teeth and the position of their eyesockets. Deer and elk, moose and rabbit and beaver, have their eyes set closer to the sides of their head, where they will be most useful. They do not need to look to the front so much as all around, to the side and rear. The lynx, the bear, the weasel, and the dog have eyes set closer to the front of the skull, where they will best serve in the pursuit. But even their eyes are not truly binocular. Only one animal around here has binocular vision, eyes set together in such a way that it can see its prey with total clarity. That animal is man."

———

THOSE WHO BELIEVE that religion causes war, apart from the historical shakiness of such claims, seem to believe that without religion human beings would lead peaceful lives. This utopian wish rests on a naïve view of who we are at our core. Hostility toward the "other" bedevils humanity, not the reality of God. Living without God does not liberate the kindness trapped inside of us. The absence of God rather licenses the hubris and cruelty of people who cannot imagine something greater than themselves. The historical evidence thus far shows that the removal of God leaves a space for destructive ideologies, not benign humanism.

The British philosopher John Gray notes, "I have been puzzled by the intensity and systematic and methodical character of the violence of the 20th century, because that century was dominated not by religious belief, but by secular belief in progress or the capacity of human beings to create a better world. It also featured unprecedented levels of mass murder." Gray puzzles over how quickly we have forgotten the lesson of secular terror and even argues that the Islamists have taken many of their methods and much of their conviction from Enlightenment radicals. Gray calls it, after the murderous avatars of the French Revolution, "Islamo-Jacobinism."

THE MODERN ISLAMIC
THREAT TO PEACE

THE FOCUS ON religious violence has been heightened by calls within fundamentalist Islam to attack the West. The prevalence of suicide bombing, faith-based threats, and the effectiveness of modern weaponry combine to make this perversion of religious faith a great danger to the world.

Some of the violence is clearly from other causes than

religious fervor. The Joint Intelligence Committee to the British Home Secretary in April 2006 cited the main causes of terrorism to be the following: opposition to war in Iraq, economic deprivation, social exclusion, and disaffection with community leaders. Those conclusions are disputable, and in the growing literature on Islam each of them has supporters and detractors. There is certainly more than religious ideology alone at work. Suicide bombing did not originate with a religious group. It was an invention of the secular Tamil Tigers and is in the murderous lineage of Japanese kamikaze pilots. Nonetheless, in modern violence there is an explicit religious motivation that is far too serious and too dangerous to be ignored.

———

AS THE WEST seeks ways to deal with Islamic radicalism, there are voices that wish to indict all faith. A dangerous manifestation of religion is not the sum of religion. Serious thought is characterized by the ability to discriminate. Islam is not monolithic. Islamic fanaticism is a great and looming threat to which the counter force should not be a wild demand to end Islam, but a call for Islamic moderation. Indonesia is the largest Muslim country in the world. Many fear that it will be radicalized. But that suggests it is currently not radicalized. Clearly there are forms of Islam that can live in peace. If fanatical Islam has recently become a threat, what was it before? Can we not encourage those whose Islamic interpretations permit coexistence to struggle against Wahhabism, the despotic Islamism that wreaks havoc both inside and outside the Islamic world?

There are Muslim countries such as Malaysia and Turkey that have not sought to export radicalism. A constitutional government, the free expression of difference, and other social arrangements can drain the venom from religious hatred. Islam itself, as many of its peaceful proponents point out, contains teachings that can redirect Islamic energies. For the West, a combination of resolution and deepened understanding is a far better program than the indiscriminate, unlearned opposition to all faith.

One powerful difference between religious fanaticism and the fanaticism of ideologies such as extreme nationalism is that religious ideas contain the seeds of their own correction. Implicit in faith is the idea of peace, of goodness, of human community. There were no resources in Nazism to correct Nazism. There are resources in Islam that moderate Muslims can deploy to change the course of radicalism.

RELIGION AS A FORCE FOR GOOD

RELIGION FUNCTIONS IN countless small ways that we tend to overlook when discussing great questions. As Michael Shermer, editor of *Skeptic* magazine, no believer himself, writes: "However, for every one of these grand tragedies there are ten thousand acts of personal kindness and social good that go unreported . . . Religion, like all social institutions of such historical depth and cultural impact, cannot be reduced to an unambiguous good or evil." In *Exodus and Revolution*, social scientist Michael Walzer reminds us how often the story of the Exodus has inspired groups fighting for their freedom. Exodus imagery motivated the Puritans arriving on these shores. In the South during slavery, images of the Bible moved people to hope for the day when they would reach "the river Jordan," that promised land of freedom.

The New Testament's ethics resonated in the social gospel of the nineteenth century. Saint Simon, the founder of French socialism who stood in opposition to the church, nonetheless extolled its practitioners:

"The men of the church were superior to the laity in their talents and virtues. It was the clergy that cleared land for cultivation, and drained unhealthy marshes; it was they who deciphered ancient manuscripts. They taught reading and writing to the lay population . . . the clergy founded the first hospitals, and the first modern institutions of learning." Those who see the medieval world as one darkened by faith might better see the medieval world as a dark one periodically enlightened by faith.

Despite the many sins committed in the name of faith, progress is often propelled by religious movements and institutions.

The civil rights movement was a religious movement.

The Southern Christian Leadership Conference, under the leadership of Reverend Martin Luther King, Jr., and in concert with many other clergy, spoke in God's name, in speeches filled with scriptural echoes, to move people to remarkable acts of courage and decency. Reverend Desmond Tutu, Elie Wiesel, and other major religious figures draw their devotion to social change from their faith. Even as religious fanaticism imperils the world, there is increasing evidence that religious decency can save it.

———

WHILE I WORKED on this book a drama unfolded in Myanmar (formerly Burma), where the clergy showed extraordinary courage and faith in the face of tyranny. From a score of such passages, here is one comment from a nonbeliever on this remarkable episode:

Ian Buruma writes, "I have never personally had either the benefits nor misfortunes of adhering to any religion, but watching Burmese monks on television defying the security forces of one of the world's most oppressive regimes, it is hard not to see some merit in religious belief." He goes on to say, "Romantics might say that Buddhism is unlike other religions, more a philosophy than a faith. But this would be untrue. It has been a religion in different parts of Asia for many centuries . . . Just as the Buddhists risked their lives to stand up for democracy in Myanmar, Christians have done so in other countries." Buruma then offers as examples the

Philippines, where the opposition of the Catholic Church doomed Marcos in 1986, and South Korea. Additionally, he notes that China has felt the power of religious opposition as well as Poland, of course, in the time of Pope John Paul II. He might have added the ecumenical protests that ended the tyranny of the Ceausescu regime in Romania in 1989.

The tremendous good that is done by faith in this world is sometimes overlooked or belittled. But most of those who are able to stand up to tyranny and hatred feel that they do so because they are empowered by a force beyond themselves.

———

IN AN UNGENEROUS passage in his book, Christopher Hitchens writes: "When the earthquake hits, or the tsunami inundates, or the Twin Towers ignite, you can see and hear the secret satisfaction of the faithful." Actually, when the tsunami struck Indonesia with catastrophic consequences, Christian aid workers were the first on the ground. The People's Church of Sri Lanka was one of the first groups to render assistance, including cleaning out the Buddhist Temple. An entire network of churches went to work, almost 1,500, more than 15 hours a day. When the Twin Towers fell, services were held in churches, synagogues— and yes, mosques—all over the world. Religion is a powerful force for good and that is why when it impels people to evil it is so jarring and ominous. As literary critic Terry

Eagleton bitingly writes of scientists: "Yet the Apocalypse is far more likely to be the product of them than the work of religion. Swap you the Inquisition for chemical warfare."

HUMAN BEINGS HAVE always dreamed of a utopia where all will be good. No such place exists. When people believe that religion makes them God's special favorites, they risk the hubris that diminishes their compassion for others. When they believe some other human system absolves them from the daily struggle to be good, because all that matters is the noble enterprise, they risk even greater evil. As that wise observer of the human condition, Alexis de Tocqueville, wrote: "As long as man has religion, he will not believe in his own perfectibility."

WE ARE, EACH of us, complex, corruptible, and sometimes noble. The anthropologist Konrad Lorenz says inside every person is a "parliament of instincts." Jumbles all, we have to question our essence. Is our central core goodness, evil, or an admixture of both? The same dilemma is posed for religion. Do Quakers or Crusaders represent the essence of Christianity? Are Sufi mystics or suicide bombers closer to the heart of Islam? Keep in mind that most of the good done in the name of religion will never be known. Each day there are endless acts of kindness, consideration, and true goodness, which are done because a religious believer is convinced that to do good is to act in harmony with God's design. And these "little, nameless, unremembered acts of kindness and of love" that the poet Wordsworth called "the best portions of a good man's life" are the legacy of faith. Physicist Freeman Dyson writes:

> "I see no way to draw up a balance sheet, to weigh the good done by religion against the evil and decide which is greater by some impartial process. My own prejudice, looking at religion from the inside, leads me to conclude that the good vastly outweighs the evil. In many places in the United States, with widening gaps between rich and poor, churches and synagogues are almost the only institutions that bind people together into communities. In church or in synagogue, people from different walks of life work together in youth groups or adult education groups, making music or teaching children, collecting money for charitable causes, and taking care of each other when sickness or disaster strikes. Without religion, the life of the country would be greatly impoverished."

Thirty years ago I stood with an old lady carrying a shopping bag at Armageddon. Then, as now, I understand that there are some people whose religious life is centered around a final battle. I also know that the site left only a vague impression on my mind, but I remember her face. The authentic impulses of faith are not those of end-time battles. The fevered dreams of triumphalism may grow from believers' disappointment, frustration, and anger, but they are not the expression of God's will in this world.

The deepest experience of God has never been in conquest but in compassion, community, holiness, and humble goodness. Inside of every human being is a battle against the pettiness and malice that thread through our character. That battle is often lost, but religion, at the very least, knows that it must be fought, and should be fought, each day of our lives.

FOUR

Does Science Disprove Religion?

A thousand years from now when scientists have solved all the questions that plague humanity, they are finally ready for the ultimate challenge. They elect a representative to address God.

"God," says the scientist in charge. "You are no longer needed. You served a function in your day, but that day is gone. We can do everything that You can do, so goodbye."

There is a moment of silence. Then a voice booms out of the sky: "Everything?"

"Yes," answers the scientist, "everything."

"Can you make a human being from dust?"

"Absolutely."

"OK," says God, "let me see you make a human being."

The scientist reaches down and digs his hands into the earth.

"Oh, no," says God. "Get your own dust."

MY CONDOLENCES

THE DISCUSSION WITH the Center for Scientific Education at Berkeley was brief and pointed. It was January of 2000, and I called them to prepare for an encounter in New York. I was scheduled to debate science and religion with Stephen Jay Gould, one of the most renowned—and quick-witted—scientists in the world. I needed to be ready.

The director of the institute returned my call and I introduced myself. "I am a rabbi and in a few months I'll be having a public debate on science and religion with Stephen Jay Gould."

There was a pause at the other end of the line. Then he spoke:

"My condolences."

———

I WAS NERVOUS going into the debate. Gould was a professor at Harvard and his essays reflected an extraordinary general range, with a wide knowledge of history, theology—everything from poetry to baseball. A renowned researcher and author, he was passionately committed to reason and modern science. He was not gentle in disagreement. I read examples of his withering dissmissiveness in debate. I cherished the hope that we could find common ground.

The assumption of many—including perhaps the organizer of the debate—was that religion was in some powerful sense opposed to science. My approach was that science and religion were complementary; science helped elaborate the wonderful workings of God's world, but hardly supplanted the need for God or damaged the religious individual's certainty of God's existence.

We did indeed find common ground. I began by telling the joke at the opening of this chapter and the debate turned into a discussion. There were no polemics, no quick jabs. One or two disagreements surfaced but on the central issue we were as one: Religion is not science, and science is not religion. Each has its joys and its own mission. Gould gave this an ornate title: NOMA, non-overlapping magisteria, a term he borrowed from the Catholic Church. In other words, neither science nor religion need trespass on the domain of the other. Scripture is not a science text and science cannot pronounce about the existence of God. In our debate he said simply, "Science and religion are different enterprises and serve different purposes in our lives. I agree with the rabbi that science is a limited domain." Gould went on to assert that science was about discovering facts and religion dealt with other "and perhaps even more important" questions such as why we are here and the purpose of the cosmos, about which, Gould insisted, science had nothing to say.

Gould did qualify a bit, and note that there are interactions between the enterprises—we do share living in the world. Throughout history, science and religion have both competed with and completed each other in many ways.

John Calvin wrote in the sixteenth century, "Scripture provides us with spectacles through which we may view the world as God's creation and self-expression; it does not, and was never intended, to provide us with an infallible repository of astronomical and medical information. The natural sciences are thus effectively emancipated from theological restrictions." The same idea was expressed by the medieval theologian and physician Maimonides 300 years before, when he insisted that a contradiction between scientific truth and scripture means that we have not properly understood scripture.

———

GOULD IS NO longer alive and cannot answer the anti-religious scientists who have followed him. Several of the recently published books arguing against faith assume that science now answers all the questions that religion once claimed as its own. They take their cue from Bertrand Russell: "We were told that faith could move mountains, but no one believed it; we are now told that the atomic bomb can remove mountains, and everyone believes it." What Russell deliberately neglects is that faith *does* move mountains, but not in the way explosives do. Faith works through human beings and its power is illustrated daily in countless lives.

Much of the supposed conflict between science and religion is what philosophers call a category mistake, like commenting on how long red is, or how educated is oatmeal—using terms that do not apply to the subject at hand. It is not quite that science teaches "how" and religion teaches "why." (The magisteria actually do overlap a bit.) My real difficulty is with the notion that science is "the only begetter of truth," as biologist Richard Lewontin once expressed it. That is both an inflated view of science and an impoverished view of truth.

THE FALSE WAR BETWEEN SCIENCE AND RELIGION

I GREW UP in a home that was a curious mix of science and religion. I am the third of four boys. My father is a rabbi, as am I and my younger brother. My oldest brother is an immunologist and the second oldest is a sociologist of medicine and a bioethicist. Discussions in our home always straddled the borders between science and religion. We were as likely to be discussing injecting mice as interpreting scripture.

Around the dinner table I learned that science was a vast, glorious tribute to the abilities God gave us to discover secrets about the created world. As I moved out of my home and encountered scientists and thinkers in the public arena, I found a dispiriting readiness to assume that religious people must oppose science, or worse, that science must demonstrate that religion is unsophisticated and ultimately untrue. That is simple-minded and wrong, and has ever been so.

It is a myth that science and religion have always been at war. This misperception is due less to history than to a few irresponsible historians. Once more Gould untangles the confusion:

> "[If] religion really did demand the suppression of important factual data at key points of contradiction with theological dogma, then how could the ranks of science include so many ordained and devoted clergymen at the highest level of respect and accomplishment—from the thirteenth-century Dominican bishop Albertus Magnus, the teacher of Thomas Aquinas and the most cogent medieval writer on scientific subjects; to Nicholas Steno, who wrote the primary works of seventeenth century geology and also became a bishop; to Lazzaro Spallanzani, the eighteenth-century Italian physiologist who disproved, by elegant experiments, the last serious arguments for spontaneous generation of life; to the Abbe Breuil, our own century's most famous student of Paleolithic cave art?"

Once we add Isaac Newton, Johannes Kepler, and even one of the fathers of evolutionary biology, Theodosius Dobzhansky, to the list of scientists who were deep believers, the commonly held picture of two opposing camps begins to blur.

Gould's judgment is not his alone. When the National Academy of Sciences issues a statement that there is no necessary conflict between science and religion, it stands on firm historical and philosophical ground.

The best known story of church-science conflict is the saga of Galileo. In 1633 the great scientist was tried for heresy for teaching that the sun, not the earth, was at the center of the world. He was found guilty, forced to recant, and placed under house arrest until the end of his life. But this is anything but a straightforward story: Before the great clash, Galileo was a good friend of the Pope's, and his astronomical assumptions were shared by prominent churchmen. Cardinal Bellarmine, who was authorized to enunciate the church's view on astronomical matters, was at first as open to new scientific discoveries as Galileo himself. During this great battle, often cited as the paradigm of the inability of science and religion to coexist, we see that misunderstandings, personal slights, insensitivities, and sheer stubbornness play as large a role as actual philosophy. Reformation historian Diarmaid MacColluch writes, "There was no clear war between 'science and religion' in the Reformation centuries . . . Around Galileo the battle lines were never simple."

Inside the religious establishment there were always those who were open to science, in Galileo's time and beyond. Darwin was laid to rest in Westminster Abbey, making a symbolic statement that needs to be heard today: faith honors those who discover truth. For people of faith to turn their back on truth, whatever its source, is a reaction of fear, not an assertion of faith.

————

SCIENCE IS A discipline that works on cumulative insight; we know more today than we did yesterday. Religion's approach to knowledge is to assimilate modern discoveries into ancient insights. The miraculousness of existence, its wonder and joy, are religious insights. As we know more about the world, that knowledge informs our response to the miracle of what exists. As Gould pointed out in our debate, the Psalmist who wrote, "the heavens declare the glory of God" (Ps. 19:1) did not actually understand how vast and intricate those heavens were. Astronomy has enlarged our appreciation of God's universe. In so doing, science augments faith; it does not diminish it.

Religion is helpful in reminding us of the truth that science, for all its virtues, is one stage of the human journey. Some people are parochial in space. They do not travel. They assume that by seeing their hometown they know all they need to know about human nature. Some people are parochial in time. They assume that by knowing their own time they know all they need to know about truth. To believe that the twenty-first century, with scientific advancement, is all we need to know about truth is to be parochial in time. We have learned much about this world, but much has been forgotten or lost. Awe and reverence are not less central to human insight than microscopes and telescopes. Scientific theories do not remain static and what we believe we know today may prove wrong or incomplete tomorrow. Truths of faith, our moral responsibility to one another, and our purpose as stewards of God's world are doctrines that endure.

The wise man, as the biologist J.B.S. Haldane taught us, regulates his conduct by the theories of both religion and science. I learned to live by Haldane's lesson. I would not treat my cancer with prayer alone and disregard the accumulated wisdom of modern medicine. Nor would I regard my body as nothing but an animate mesh of gears and wires. I took medicine *and* prayed; submitted to tests *and* believed that there is a purpose to things, intelligible or mysterious. Cancer and its treatment were to be not only endured but also explored. I knew that creating meaning was as important as submitting to the medicinal regime, and that meaning is a gift of increased sensitivity, understanding, and compassion. Science and spirit are not opposed. They join hands in our lives, often to save them. They did in mine.

———

WHEN ANYONE, WHETHER a scientist or a chimney sweep, says that God created the world or God did not create the world, that person is not making a scientific assertion. Microscopes and telescopes will not show God, and the assertion of scientists that science can prove or disprove God is foolish. God is not a scientific problem. But as the psychologist Abraham Maslow wrote, if the only tool you have is a hammer, every problem tends to look like a nail.

DO WE HAVE MINDS?

WE KNOW WE have brains, which are measurable and material, but do we have minds, which are neither? Nobel Prize-winning neurologist Sir John Eccles wrote that "we are beings with souls in a spiritual world, as well as material beings with bodies and brains existing in a material world." This conclusion arose from his reflections on the puzzling, ancient question of how we have minds. What makes us self-conscious?

Consciousness is part of this debate because of the dogma of materialism. There exists a firm belief among some scientists that nothing exists apart from matter. This is not provable, but it is often assumed. The idea that there is nothing but matter (or as some refer to it, stuff), and everything emerges from matter, is at odds with much of what we experience, believe, and know. How do we get from the material to the nonmaterial? How does a brain, which shares the same molecules as a rock and a desk, produce an idea?

The surgeon Richard Selzer wrote that "The surgeon knows all the parts of the brain but he does not know the patient's dreams." The surgeon does not know the night dreams of the patient, and his joys, his frustrations, his dreams for life remain opaque as well. Dreams are mysterious to the surgeon, but to the one who believes that we are only matter they must be positively baffling. For dreams not only exist in our own minds, they can actually change the minds of others. If I tell you my dream, and your ideas change as a result, then something nonmaterial—a dream and a word—has changed something material—a brain. Actions that are a result of brain chemistry change in response to words, to dreams, to intangible things. Recent studies demonstrate that culture changes the way in which our brains are hardwired. The nonphysical world changes the physical world.

For the religious individual this is not an enigma but an analogy; it is how God interacts with the world. God is nonphysical and nonmeasurable but changes the world we experience. Consciousness, far from being an illusion or an "epiphenomena" (that is, a by-product of other things), is the gift we have to reach toward God. Faith proposes a connection of the nonmaterial: You may sit and pray silently. No one can hear you; no one can see your prayer. Yet God, equally unseen, listens.

HOW DOES MATTER
FIGURE ITSELF OUT?

CHARLES DARWIN HIMSELF states the problem succinctly: "Can the mind of man, which has, as I fully believe, been developed from a mind as low as that possessed by the lowest animals, be trusted when it draws such grand conclusions?"

Darwin's question remains unanswered: How can stuff randomly assembled or selected by blind forces through millions of years arrive at true conclusions about the nature of the universe? Materialism itself requires an extraordinary leap of faith: Why believe our discoveries about the universe if our brains are evolved matter with no design or spirit that makes them capable of comprehension? Einstein writes that "the most incomprehensible thing about the universe is that it is comprehensible." Understanding makes most sense as a statement of faith that God fashioned the universe in such a way as to match our minds to its laws.

Our inability to understand consciousness and how evolved matter can comprehend the universe should induce a little humility. As maturity in an individual consists in recognizing his own limitations, so maturity in a thinker is often marked by admitting certain features of the world cannot be understood.

Human reason is limited as all human faculties are limited. We cannot lift buildings or see across continents: Our physical strength is slight, our senses are imperfect. It is easy to forget that our reason is similarly limited. Surely with a touch of imagination, and a touch less arrogance, we can appreciate that there is much in this world, its creation, governance, and majesty, that we do not begin to understand. The blessing of consciousness does not bring with it the faculty of omniscience.

EVOLUTION AND FAITH

EVOLUTION EXPLAINS A great deal about development in humans and other species, our physical structure, internal systems, and even much of our behavior. What it does *not* explain is the force that propels evolution itself. What secret sets the selection in motion? What is, in the language of poet Dylan Thomas, "The force that through the green fuse drives the flower?"

Is evolution compatible with faith? Stephen Jay Gould's characteristically tart answer should suffice: "Either half my colleagues are enormously stupid, or else the science of Darwinism is fully compatible with conventional religious beliefs—and equally compatible with atheism."

Evolution describes the way the world was made and continues to be made. A professor of biology, Ken Miller, quotes a teacher's remark that more impressive than watching a pool player make a single shot to sink fifteen separate balls is watching him hit the cue ball, which hits a second ball and a third, all in sequence until the table is cleared. Evolution is a complex shot that accomplished many things over long stretches of time. The atheistic assumption that all is random is a statement of faith in disbelief, not of scientific veracity. Francis Collins, Director of the Human Genome Project, writes about the discovery of the genome and its attendant wonders: "For those who believe in God, there are reasons now to be more in awe, not less."

Insights from evolution do make a contribution to the study of religion. They can help explain why some religions have more success in spreading their message, or make clear the strategies that enable religion to help its followers cope with the world. Additionally, evolution teaches that the world is in a continuous process of self-creation. The Biblical story of creation has God saying, "Let us make man." Biblical commentators fancifully infer that God is speaking to the human being about to be created, saying, "Together we will shape what you become." Evolution reminds us of the dynamic nature of all creation. Everything is in motion, creation is continuous, and our choices are crucial to the unfolding of the future.

Human beings retain the capacity to grow. Once other animals reach adolescence, they have fulfilled their potential for growth. Human beings do not cease acquiring wisdom; at least they *need* not cease acquiring wisdom, throughout life. Part of everything, we also stand apart from everything.

As much as evolution ties us to all life, religious thought reminds us that we are also distinct from other creatures. Instinct governs animal life; human beings can transcend their own inclinations. In my freshman class in psychology the professor pointed out that knowing a psychological rule can invalidate it. There is a rule in mass psychology that the greater the number of people who witness a crisis, the less likely any individual is to get involved. If you see a crime on the street and there are many people around, you are unlikely to intervene because you will count on others. But, he continued, now that you know the rule, you will be more likely to step forward. Knowing the law, you can violate it.

Human beings make mockery of Darwinian certainties every day. What are we supposed to care about? On a deep level, on the level of our genes, it is reproduction that rules us. As we have pointed out, however, affluent couples limit their offspring or choose not to have children—indeed at times choose celibacy, preferring travel, cultural enrichment, and so forth—over the presumed Darwinian raison d'être. In other words, the drive to pass on our genes, which would be sovereign if we were but animals, can be subordinated to other things. "A man's reach," as Browning wrote, "should exceed his grasp/ Or what's a heaven for?" The certainty of something beyond us moves us to be greater than ourselves, to push past the confines of biology. Animals we may be, but we are not only animals.

ALTRUISM

MY PATERNAL GRANDFATHER died when my father was eleven years old. His mother was a widow at thirty-four, and he—an only child—bore much of his grief alone. In accordance with traditional Jewish practice, he began to walk very early to synagogue each morning to say prayers in his father's memory, a practice lasting for a year after a parent's death.

At the end of his first week, he noticed that the ritual director of the synagogue, Mr. Einstein, walked past his home just as he left to walk to synagogue. Mr. Einstein, already advanced in years, explained, "Your home is on the way to the synagogue. I thought it might be fun to have some company. That way, I don't have to walk alone."

For a year my father and Mr. Einstein walked through the New England seasons, the humidity of summer and the snow of winter. They talked about life and loss and for a while my father was not so alone.

After my parents married and my oldest brother was born, my father called Mr. Einstein, now well into his nineties, and asked if he would like to meet my father's new wife and child. Mr. Einstein agreed, but said that in view of his age my father would have to come to him. My father writes:

"The journey was long and complicated. His home, by car, was fully twenty minutes away. I drove in tears as I realized what he had done. He had walked for an hour to my home so that I would not have to be alone each morning . . . By the simplest of gestures, the act of caring, he took a frightened child and he led him with confidence and with faith back into life."

———

WHAT POSSIBLE EXPLANATION is there for a person who spends her time, resources, and skills helping another? According to evolutionary theory, if that person is a relative there is a ready explanation: it is nature's subtle way of perpetuating the gene pool. I will sacrifice myself for my child because she carries my genes.

But why would I throw myself on a grenade to save someone whom I do not know? Or donate a kidney, or bother to give blood?

The evolutionary biologist William Hamilton arrived at "Hamilton's Rule," which states that there is a mathematical formula to calculate the cost of the act and the closeness of the actor and beneficiary. The "currency" is children, or genes. (Renowned biologist J. B. S. Haldane wryly commented that he would sacrifice himself to save two brothers or eight cousins.) Our genes (without our being conscious of it) are programmed to act on behalf of those who share our genetic material. The more they share, the greater the motivation to care for them, even sacrifice for them. Can this really explain all the selfless acts done by people all over the world? How could selflessness be the summit of human attainment, when it is directly contrary to what nature, in its all powerful and subtle ways, dictates for us?

The easy explanation, powerfully resisted, is that there is something greater than just genes to which our spirit responds. We are called to goodness not through evolutionary ingenuity alone but through the soul's pointing upward, as the compass needle is moved by magnetism. We respond to forces that cannot be seen and are nonmaterial. Here is what evolution does not do: turn sex to love, fear to friendship, puzzlement to purpose, desire to sanctification. With God's inspiration and aid, urging us on and giving us guidance, human beings do all that.

The Psalmist writes (Ps. 37:3) "Trust in God and do good." Notice the sequence; sometimes, the trust is what motivates us to do good.

Explaining altruism purely as a product of evolution is similar to other, now discredited explanations of human behavior. In the early twentieth century one school of thought taught that all our decisions were the result of class struggle. Another taught they were all a product of childhood experiences. Now we learn that in fact it is all about genes. A theory that reduces human kindness to DNA may in the end tell us less about kindness than about the assumptions of the theorist.

Religion is not disproved by explaining how it came to be. One can study its origins and still hold fast to its teachings. An evolutionary scientist can also be a believer.

As one of the most noted evolutionary theorists in this field, David Sloan Wilson writes in his book *Darwin's Cathedral: Evolution, Religion and the Nature of Society*, "A very high proportion of scientists themselves profess a belief in God and participate in organized religions . . . Clearly, we must think of religious thought as something that coexists with scientific thought, not as an inferior version of it."

THE SHAPE OF THE COSMOS

Is our world uniquely designed for life? This is a raging debate among cosmologists, with distinguished names ranging on both sides. How did order first enter the world when we know from the second law of thermodynamics that systems become increasingly disordered? Are there other places that support life?

At issue is the anthropic principle, which is a hotly debated subject in modern physics. "Anthropic coincidences" are certain features of the laws of physics that seem exactly what is needed for life to exist. One physicist puts it this way: "The universe and its laws seem in some respects to be balanced on a knife edge." These coincidences, although variously explained by scientists, when taken together are referred to by some as "the anthropic principle."

Many physicists do not believe that life arose purely by chance. As Paul Davies writes, "If the universe is simply an accident, the odds against it containing any appreciable order are ludicrously small."

The more we look at the many spectacularly ordered facets of our universe, the harder it is to credit them to chance. A physics professor at Yale, William R. Bennett, has calculated that if a trillion monkeys typed ten random characters a second, it would still take a trillion times longer than the universe has been in existence to produce the sentence "To be or not to be, that is the question."

Conditions had to be exquisitely finely tuned in order for life to arise on planet Earth. Physicists give different accounts of such necessary conditions, but in every instance the numbers are staggering indeed.

In his book *Just Six Numbers*, the Astronomer Royal Sir Martin Rees offers six numbers that "constitute a recipe for the universe." Each number is perfectly gauged to permit life on earth. Rees continues, " . . . if any one of them were to be 'untuned,' there would be no stars and no life. Is this tuning just a brute fact, a coincidence? Or is it the providence of a benign Creator?" Rees himself endorses neither conclusion.

Donald Page of Princeton's Institute for Advanced Study has calculated the odds against the formation of our universe as 1 out of 10,000,000[124].

Other physicists assume the meaningfulness of this remarkable attunement. Stephen Barr, Professor of Physics at the University of Delaware, writes of eleven such "anthropic coincidences," as he calls them. Included, for example, is the "cosmological constant," which tells how much gravitational pull is exerted by empty space. The number is 10^{-120}. This is, as Barr notes, "an amazingly small number." Were it not so small, he writes, the universe would "not have been able to have a nice steady existence for the billions of years required for life to evolve."

While a non-scientist cannot adjudicate between the two camps—and indeed no single scientist can claim to be certain—one thing is clear. The idea that this world is finely tuned for life is both scientifically plausible and consistent with theism. Echoing Barr above, Francis Collins writes that "the existence of the universe as we know it rests upon a knife edge of improbability." The knife-edged constants that permit us to flourish in this small corner of the universe have not, to our knowledge, been reproduced elsewhere.

The anthropic principle was the occasion of the major disagreement in my debate with Stephen Jay Gould, mentioned at the opening of this chapter. He insisted that it was an abuse of probability theory to claim that a unique occurrence was remarkable *after* it happened. For once it has occurred, as the one result in billions that might have happened, the observer would claim uniqueness for *any* result. You can drop a million coins and whichever way they land would be unlikely before you dropped them. This argument has been echoed by others who correctly point out that had the universe not come so astonishingly into being we would not be here to celebrate it anyway.

Even if it is true that no matter what attributes the universe displayed one could say it was remarkable, it removes the argument for the world being designed, but makes no case that it wasn't. But in fact Gould may be incorrect. One theologian counters with the example of a man facing a firing squad of twenty sharpshooters. If they all miss, it is true that only then would the intended victim live to tell how remarkable was the event, but that does not mean it wouldn't be remarkable. After all, if you dropped those million coins and they all landed heads up, you would be entitled to wonder if there had been some kind of intervention. If we see this world as an astonishing wonder, on an order far more miraculous than a million coins landing on the same side, then intervention is a compelling conclusion.

The debate over the plausibility of the anthropic principle illustrates a question of attitude that threads through the larger debate over God's existence.

Since there can be no certainty that God does not exist— the most one can say is that there is no *evidence* of God—

why are some so adamant in denying the possibility? The vigor with which some scientists reject God is attributable to qualities other than scientific rigor. Religion arouses the ire of some; its doctrines call for a certain way of life, and its history can be variously interpreted. It is easy to understand why specific religions are criticized or rejected. But why one would be so angry about the very idea that God might exist?

Some light is shed by a confession offered by the philosopher Thomas Nagel. This perceptive passage deserves to be quoted in full:

> "I want atheism to be true and am made uneasy by the fact that some of the most intelligent and well-informed people I know are religious believers. It isn't just that I don't believe in God and, naturally, hope that I'm right in my belief. It's that I hope there is no God! I don't want there to be a God; I don't want the universe to be like that.
>
> "My guess is that this cosmic authority problem is not a rare condition and that it is responsible for much of the scientism and reductionism of our time. One of the tendencies it supports is the ludicrous overuse of evolutionary biology to explain everything about life, including everything about the human mind."

While applauding Nagel's honesty, one is entitled to speculate on the origins of his discomfort. Why should someone *wish* for there to be no God? Just such a craving for what Harvard physicist Owen Gingerich in his book *God's Universe* calls "the gospel of meaninglessness" moves some physicists not merely to doubt that God designed the world, but to *assert* that God did not. Such a claim is not science.

Scientists tend to be independent and trusting of the abilities of human intellect. Religion encourages a humble acceptance of limitations. The mind is a gift; it is extraordinary; but it is slight beside the power that endows all with life and purpose.

Inside all of us is a single-mindedness that disdains the authority of others. Whether this is resilience or rebellion will depend upon our view of the human spirit. Without courage, human beings would long since have perished. But pluck is akin to pride, and determination akin to hubris. Wishing for a world without God misapprehends belief. Living with God is not living with a divine dictatorship. Dictators do not create and love you. Dictatorships do not cultivate the human capacity for forgiveness and goodness. Dictators do not fashion a world miraculously endowed with creations that can discover its laws. A belief in God makes demands, but they are demands that both enlarge and refine the human spirit.

MONOTHEISM AND SCIENCE

RELIGIOUS BELIEF FUELED the creativity of Western civilization. Monotheistic traditions teach that God made an ordered world, a world that can be understood, a world that can be improved by human effort. Historian Daniel Boorstin attributes the technological superiority of the West to the idea of a creator God. This is also the view of Sir Isaac Newton, who believed that science flourished best in monotheistic cultures. Newton spent a great deal of time interpreting scripture. He believed that religious scholarship and his scientific discoveries were not in opposition to one another but were different facets of uncovering the truths in God's word and God's world.

As the physicist Robert Jastrow famously remarked, "At this moment it seems as though science will never be able to raise the curtain on the mystery of creation. For the scientist who has lived by his faith in the power of reason, the story ends like a bad dream. He has scaled the mountains of ignorance; he is about to conquer the highest peak; as he pulls himself over the final rock, he is greeted by a band of theologians who have been sitting there for centuries."

———

DOES BELIEVING IN God help even science make more sense? In my family, that was certainly the case. Never did my brothers' researches suggest that because the secrets of immunology were being unraveled, God was dispensable. Rather, the exhilarating miracle that we are here, that the world exists and yields its secrets, is the framework upon which all of science was constructed.

———

PAUL DAVIES REPORTS that he has asked many of his colleagues why the laws of physics are what they are. The answers vary from "That's not a scientific question" to "Nobody knows" to "There is no reason they are what they are—they just are." Davies continues, "The idea that laws exist reasonlessly is deeply anti-rational . . . the very notion of physical law is a theological one in the first place, a fact that makes many scientists squirm." There is another way to see this astonishing beneficence. In the practice of science itself is a kind of piety that can rejoice and be grateful for such a gift.

Each human being, scientist or not, stands before life with the same questions. Baffled by the brief passage through this world, at a certain age we are all subject to concerns that transcend what we know, and take root in what we believe. I cannot count the times I have sat beside the bed of a person facing death who tells me he is uncertain about faith in God but still needs to know why. "Why"—why is this happening to me, why can I not figure out the twists of fate, why do I need to find meaning in my destiny—is the question that will not leave us alone, no matter how conflicted our faith.

Less than two years after my dialogue with Stephen Jay Gould, he died of cancer. He said nothing about his recurring battle with cancer the evening we met. He had been diagnosed with mesothelioma two decades before and written a clear-eyed paper about the misleading nature of cancer statistics. At the time he was first diagnosed he was given less than a year to live, but twenty years later he died of an unrelated cancer. There was a reception after the event where we spoke for a while about many things. He recounted his various battles with scientists over questions of religion. We talked about how deeply he loved religious architecture and art. As I was about to leave, he asked about my books. I described them and he asked, "Which is the most theological?" I answered that it was my first, *The Healer of Shattered Hearts: A Jewish View of God.* "Send me a copy," he said, "I like to read theology."

Gould, who wrote such elegant essays on the history of science, believed in learning from many sources. We live in a time when science and religion do not speak to each other nearly as much as they ought to, or as much as they could. On each side are polemicists who dismiss the seriousness and worthiness of the other. Gould's openness is a legacy worth honoring in a divided age.

FIVE

What Does Religion Really Teach?

"A little philosophy inclineth a man's mind to atheism; but depth in philosophy bringeth men's minds to religion."

Francis Bacon, *Essays XVI*

THE FIRST DECADE after becoming a rabbi I avoided taking a job in a congregation, choosing instead to teach. I still teach periodically at a university, in large part because talking to students is a refresher course for the questions that moved me along my path at the outset. For me, choosing to stay in the classroom was at first a way of maintaining a distance from others. It helped me feel safe. I did not need to be too involved in my students' lives. There was a new class each year, and at the end of the year both the students and I moved on.

College and graduate school is a specialized and limited world. It is intellectually enriching, but a great deal of life remains outside the classroom, untouched by the debates within. In the years I was engaged in teaching alone, I never performed the tasks and ceremonies of most clergy: weddings, funerals, counseling. So it was a new experience for me when, in the first days as a synagogue rabbi, I was called in to visit a woman on her deathbed. Her family, distraught, explained that she was in her last days, in a coma, and asked me to say a prayer. Arriving at the hospital I saw them gathered around the bed. I explained that the appropriate prayer was the final confessional, called in Hebrew "a vidui." They left me alone with her.

I had never said a deathbed prayer before. I did not know the woman, who lay with her eyes closed, entangled in tubes and wires. As I looked at her and contemplated my task I felt like a fraud. Who was I to take in my hands this responsibility? She was unknown to me in life, and now on the edge of death it should be someone older, wiser, better than I to usher her into eternity.

I was grateful that she was not aware of her surroundings. Perhaps she would not realize quite how uncertain I was. Were she awake she would feel my cold hand, lose confidence in me, and perhaps in that delicate moment, despair of the tradition or even of God. But she lay unconscious as I held her hand and began to recite the prayer. The power of the words vied with my unease, giving me some sense of accomplishment despite my anxiety. Having completed the prayer, I silently asked her forgiveness, spoke with the family, and left.

That night I came home and my wife asked me how it went. I told her I felt like a fraud, that I had an overwhelming sense that I was not up to shepherding a soul in its final moments on earth. Who am I to be doing this? I felt unworthy.

You are right, she said. You are unworthy. Anyone would be unworthy. But it is ok, because *you* are not doing it. It is being done *through* you.

That was a pivotal moment for me. Suddenly it became clear to me that we bring light into this world not as a source but as a prism—it comes *through* us. As electricity requires a conduit, so spirit moves through human beings to touch others in crucial moments. When the ceremony was about me, I could not bear it. My discomfort may seem like humility but it is really ego; I made the experience about my unworthiness rather than about God, or the person lying before me. As soon as I stepped out of my own way, the prayer felt real. I could believe in blessing when I felt that it did not depend upon me. A musician translates the notes on the page into music; she is not their source, but their medium.

God is both beyond and within a human being, the God of the sky and of the soul. Each individual can act as a channel for God's goodness, and each religious tradition teaches ways that goodness can be realized in the world. The story of standing by a dying person's bed is not a Jewish story, or a Christian story, or a Muslim story; it is a story of two people before God, a story of faith.

———

THE MONOTHEISTIC FAITHS share many such stories. In philosophy there are divergent schools called "lumpers" and "splitters." One type of thinker specializes in putting things together, seeing their similarities, and another pries them apart, focusing on differences. The splitters emphasize the differences between religions. There are many and important differences, to be sure. But as the story above reminds us, there is much that we share, and in this chapter we cast our lot with the lumpers, and look for the key teachings common to the monotheistic faiths. Each great faith gives expression in its way to certain eternal truths.

THE SEASHELL THEORY

CHILDREN DELIGHT IN putting a seashell to their ears. Listening, they hear magically the rush and roar of the waves. What they do not know, of course, is that they are listening to the rushing blood inside their own heads.

Atheistic theories about religion are seashell theories. Faith begins in our imaginations, or in our fears, and we then believe we are hearing the true currents of the universe. Those who believe they hear most clearly are indeed the most deceived. What makes someone into a prophet? The seashell theory of prophecy is that there is no receiving, only inventing. The prophet hears nothing, but mistakenly believes he does.

All the monotheistic faiths reject the seashell theory—the idea that God is just the sound of our own yearning echoing through the universe. Believers deny that religion is, in the end, only about us. Religion insists that there is a nonmaterial realm accessible to us. We do not always understand it properly; listening is at least as difficult an art as painting, writing, or music. Yet the sounds of faith are not hallucinatory echoes but genuine calls to holy living in this world.

There are beliefs about the universe and human nature, about prayer, about tradition and moral meaning, about our purpose on earth and our ultimate destiny, that are central to that call.

A SUPERINTENDED UNIVERSE, AN UNDERSTOOD SOUL

ARE WE ALONE?

———

ASTRONOMERS SEND SETI probes into the cosmos, hoping to establish contact with life on another planet. Perhaps one day we will establish such communication; the universe is vast and it may be that there is life outside our small corner. Until that moment we all wonder if we are alone.

The sense of being alone begins early in life. Child psychologists teach us that to an infant, the parent somehow exists "inside" the child. The hungry infant cries, the breast appears. Then one day the child learns to say that terrifying, wonderful word "I." (The German philosopher Fichte celebrated his children's births not on the anniversary of the day they were born, but the anniversary of the day they first said "I.") "I" means "not you." On the day we first say "I" we learn to keep secrets, and build an inner world. We also realize that inside ourselves, we are alone.

On a typical day you go out into the world. You have thousands of experiences, thoughts, dreams, wisps of memory and anticipation. You have conversations, feel frustrated or glad, learn a bit more about others and about the world. Then you come home and your spouse asks, "How was your day?" and you answer, "Fine." All that you thought and heard and saw, that vast parade of images and memories, is lost. At most you can communicate a small fraction of the experience of your life. Inside yourself you are alone.

As a believer, however, I am never fully isolated in this world. What I forget, God remembers. What I experience, God understands. The world may be cruel, but it is never empty. I may feel despondent, but I am never alone.

The philosopher Jean-Paul Sartre struggled with questions of faith and unbelief his entire life. He once compared his search for God to a man sitting in a café waiting for his friend. People come and go, but the man remains focused only on the appearance of his friend. The people who walk in, barely noticed, are less real in his mind than the absence of the one for whom he is waiting.

In all my years of seeking, God actually *was* close. My search kept beside me the presence of One in whom I did not believe. I know that sounds strange, but many people find even the sense of God's absence more real than the presence of many other things in the world. There is a God-sized hole in their lives. The seashell theory assumes it is a psychological deficiency, that we crave God not because there is a God but because we fear, or hope. Actually it is not a delusion but a response, a reaching toward what is most real. People who search for love are familiar with the feeling; they are looking for a powerful, real bond; as with the friend in the café, it is a waiting for a presence that is known to exist. The task for one who feels God's absence is not to prove God, but to find God.

So as I looked for God on the streets of Jerusalem, or in the mountains of Scotland, or in the forests of California, I was not passionless. It was not a cold search. Even the vigor of my atheism was a testament to how deeply I cared. Indifference distances us from God. The angry spirit, on the other hand, is not far from the seeking spirit; only for the passionless is there no path.

The desire for God is a deep one. As with other essential needs, it has a genuine means of satisfaction. What we need for life actually does exist: Satisfying the need for food, there is bread. Satisfying the need for rest, there is sleep. Satisfying the need for expression, there is language. Satisfying the need for transcendence, there is the presence of the One.

GIFTS OF FAITH

LOOKING UP AT the night sky is frightening and promising. Does it show emptiness or the sparkle of design? In the years when I denied the possibility of God, I felt my view of an empty cosmos carried a sort of dull glow of courage; I could face the world without supernatural support. The image of the proud atheist on a solitary march is stirring. But it may be more true to say with Harry Emerson Fosdick that atheism is the theoretical formulation of a discouraged life.

To discover God's presence is at the same time to recognize a world charged with meaning, alive with the certainty of purpose. This place is filled with "swift, slow; sweet, sour; adazzle, dim," all things, as the poet Hopkins writes, that God "fathers forth." There is a poetry that is conferred by faith, because the world is a coherent and intended work of art. Belief is not the child of hope. Belief bestows hope.

Beauty, coherence, and hope are the gifts of belief. Believing opens our eyes—how we approach the world determines what we find in it. The world's beauty vanishes in moments of discouragement. It is restored in times of hope. This is true in human relationships as well as relationship to God.

For years I have conducted worship services for singles, both in Philadelphia and now in Los Angeles. Most of the people come with the hope that they will meet someone. Neither I nor anyone else can tell with certainty who will be successful. But I can usually tell who will not. A sullen attitude, a lack of excitement about oneself and others, an unwillingness to listen—all of these are almost foolproof indicators that the individual will leave alone. Love rarely finds the one encased in armor.

What is true of human beings is true of God. How can I meet God if I venture out into the world weighed down by the purposelessness and emptiness of it all? To be open, to be humble, to seek—these are the preconditions to find something that simple reason alone will never yield. Deuteronomy 6:6 reads, "and these words which I command you this day shall be on your heart." The Rabbi of Kotzk, a nineteenth-century teacher, asked why the Bible states "on your heart" when it really wishes the words to be "in your heart." His answer is that hearts are not always open. But if you place the words on your heart, when the heart is more receptive, they will sink in and there unfold their deeper meaning. This is true of all great messages in life, which take on their deeper shades only when we are ready. Clichés that mean nothing in youth suddenly become profundities as we age. Similarly, the idea of God can seem pale and distant when we are remote from sources of spirit. Later, a moment of faithful intimacy can change our lives forever.

Devotional literature, prayer, a religious community, an appreciation of the wonders of the natural world, an open heart to the testimonies of others, can help develop our capacity for faith. We develop that capacity not through argument but through openness: Two people look at the same ocean; one is spurred to poetry. Two people look at the same sky; one is called to prayer. The difference is not in the weight of evidence, but in the receptivity of soul.

There is a story of a Hasidic rabbi whose child used to wander off to spend time alone in a forest. Concerned and curious, one day the rabbi pulled his boy aside to ask him what he was doing. "I go to the forest to find God," said the boy. "That's wonderful," replied his father. "But you need not go to the forest to find God. Don't you know that God is the same everywhere?" "God is," the boy answered, "but I'm not."

Placing ourselves with people or in situations where we feel closer to God's presence is a means of opening a receptive soul. I find God in a quiet moment, or sometimes in the midst of a raucous, engaged congregation. God is present when at a funeral I hear someone's life being honored by a spouse or a child and at a wedding when I see that there is between the couple both love and a deep faith.

These experiences show me a world that is superintended, under God's providential care. And the same God who fashioned the cosmos sees into the soul. Without God we are orphans in the cosmos. Bertrand Russell's essay "A Free Man's Worship" describes life as follows: "The life of Man is a long march through the night, surrounded by invisible foes, tortured by weariness and pain, towards a goal that few can hope to reach, and where none may tarry long. One by one, as they march, our comrades vanish from our sight, seized by the silent orders of omnipotent Death."

In such a bleak world view, the belief that there is a face to the cosmos is as arbitrary and illusory as the belief that there is a face in the clouds. The world promises nothing. Nothing is the backdrop from which we came and to which we will return. What meaning and purpose—fleeting and small—we wrest from this earth is our own.

That is not the world I experience: Instead, I see a world of more coherence than chaos. Life is filled with opportunities to create beauty, to forge meaning; recently reported studies show an increase in happiness among those who contribute to charities, reinforcing the idea that when we help, the world makes sense—our own lives come together. God has given us the power to assemble the separate pieces of our own stories and shape a pattern. When the pattern seems elusive, or impossible to discern, the fault may lie not in life, but in our powers of apprehension. We may be look-ing at the back of the carpet, seeing loose strings and unfinished leads, whereas a view of the second side would show a weave of intricate beauty.

Even knowing that we cannot see things whole, at times belief carries with it an additional burden. The very certainty of God's care heightens frustration with inequities and cruelties in the world. As a believer, I still experience the world in anguished moments as Russell describes it, indifferent or even hostile.

DOES SUPERINTENDENCE MAKE A PERFECT WORLD?

THE WORLD IS unfair. Anyone who denies that premise is forced into callousness ("you deserved that") and false certainties ("suffering is always for a good reason, even if we don't understand it"). A child born in a relocation camp in sub-Saharan Africa who will suffer and die is born into an unfair world. Did I "deserve" to be born to loving parents in the richest country in the world while that child was born into deadly poverty? There is no moral calculus that can make that fit any notion of justice the human mind might comprehend. Against the backdrop of such injustice, Russell's pessimism strikes a receptive chord in us.

My mother's stroke at age fifty-two shattered my parents' lives. My mother, who was a university administrator, a fundraiser, a teacher, could now not speak, could not write, could barely read a sentence. The stroke had stolen her words.

There were other aspects to her sudden illness: an emotionality that resulted in tremendous rage; the bewilderment and the pain of being betrayed by her own body. But those agonies were small compared to the inability to explain what she felt, to give voice to what was going on inside her. Expressive aphasia impairs or destroys the ability to speak. At times when words can be spoken, the ability to form sentences is lost. Syntax is garbled, the wrong words present themselves, simple expressions are mislaid in the mind and cannot be retrieved.

Occasionally a word would emerge, one word to explain the horror of her condition. Early on, after a good deal of struggle, she managed to pronounce something she had been trying to say for some time: "Prison." She repeated it again and again with a sort of mantric regularity. It became an anchor, as other words would in the future. Prison. Prison. Prison.

My mother taught me and my brothers how to read. Now she will never ask casually for the newspaper to be passed across the breakfast table, or speed unthinkingly through a mystery novel, or make conversation unpunctuated by long pauses, a painful groping for a phrase, a frustration with her lot. It is a fate she will not forgive and cannot change.

My mother's story is unique, as are all stories of human suffering, but it is also shared. Everyone comes to know unfairness, the twist of painful fate that upends a life. We are tempted to find reasons, but reasons ring hollow in the presence of one in pain.

Yet a conviction of the world's unfairness is not the same as a conviction there is no God. As a rabbi, hearing almost daily of the tragedies in our community, I don't need the nightly news to tell me how deeply unfair is the world in which we live. The day I write these words, a child in my congregation is receiving an operation on the other side of the country where a specialist will—if all goes well— succeed in leaving him only mildly disabled. He is still too young to appreciate what is happening; his parents had to choose the operation for him. In their eyes, courageous though they are, is all the truth about the world's unfairness one ever need know.

Can one be clear-eyed about the world's cruelties and still believe in its superintendence? From our partial under-standing, even in the midst of sorrow, I believe we can find a small glimpse of a promise that is lasting.

Through all the interconnections of the world I see a work of art. I write that not as a testable hypothesis but a spiritual certainty. How such beauty can be reconciled with the squalor and pain of an unfair world is the great chal-lenge of faith. The first step in understanding the world is to understand ourselves. How we see the world cannot be separated from our view of human beings. The Bible declares that we are created in the image of God. What can that mean, and in what way does it help answer our perplexities?

IMAGE OF GOD

AT THE OUTSET of creation (Gen. 1:27), the Bible teaches that human beings are made in God's image. Can one be in the image of that which is not physical? Along with God's existence, this idea of human beings as lifted above nature, in God's image, is the fundamental religious truth that is under most serious attack.

Some modern historians teach that Darwin robbed us of the idea of our uniqueness. Believing we were special creations, evolution taught us that we were not. Since then, confidence in God's relation to human beings has faded, for to be in the image of God cannot mean that 1 percent of our DNA is different from that of a chimpanzee.

———

STANDING WITHIN THE matrix of the world, however, does not rob us of specialness. Small differences are decisive. As we saw in the previous chapter, the very existence of our world is balanced on tiny cosmological constants. If they were just a bit different we would perish. To be genetically similar is not an argument against being unique. At times a vast machinery exists to produce a single astonishing result.

Physicist John Wheeler, explaining how the universe created our single planet, speaks of giant plants that exist to bring forth a single flower. Similarly the vast array of nature brings forth the human being from within. Our kinship with the natural world means we are of it, but we are also, like the flower, unlike all else.

One of religion's most important affirmations is the relatedness of all human beings. The Bible does not begin with a certain tribe or group being in God's image. Adam and Eve are not members of any group except humanity. Pride, pugnacity, and human limitations have always persuaded one group that they are better or higher than another, yet the teaching is unambiguous; at the beginning of the Bible it is the human being, of no specified race or culture, who is made in God's image.

This image is the spark of eternity within each person, what is often called the soul. This is precisely the part of the human being one cannot point to, which is not physically described or describable.

That image can be violated or betrayed, but it cannot be erased.

Being in God's image means we are morally responsible. What criteria do we use when we say that Stalin was evil? If Darwinian, he was a successful animal, predominant over his group and surviving until his bodily organism gave way. (Maybe it is no coincidence that as a youth, Stalin urged copies of Darwin on his friends to prove there was no God.) We may not like the effect he had on the entirety of the species, but so what? Why should we like it any more than we like dominant animals who destroy others? Because we hold humanity to a different standard. Because our moral obligation is to all humanity, not just to self-advancement. Such a conclusion is well beyond what our genes can dictate or plead. Suddenly the image of God has crept in; we should be better because we are not merely animals. We are something greater.

Stalin too was in God's image—that is precisely why we can say that he violated, in the grossest way, that image. Human beings can be demonic because they have the potential to be godly. You can only betray a standard if you have the potential to fulfill it. All human beings are called to decency. We do not demand decency of animals. If we are animals alone, how can we really be judged?

Human beings organize themselves into castes, tribes, groups, different identities. Underneath it all we share not only a genetic similarity, but also a common humanity.

For years I have tried the following exercise with groups across the country. In explaining the image of God, I tell them that it is not physical, yet what represents God in this world best is neither the sky nor the sanctuary, but the human face. "Look into the eyes of the person sitting next to you and you will see an image of God." Then, people will look at those sitting next to them, and they will smile.

In explaining why this happens, I point to the tremendous emotional power in looking into the eyes of the person sitting next to you. It takes people by surprise. They are not ready for it. When we are faced with a strong emotion and we wish to minimize it, we smile, or we make a joke. As Nieztsche wrote, "Wit closes the coffin on an emotion." When you are moved, and wish the feeling to go away, laugh. Later on, I urge the groups to whom I speak, when you are not sitting in a lecture, look into that person's eyes again and do not let yourself laugh. You will feel the electric current of spirit that runs from one person to another in God's world.

To be in God's image is to understand that there is part of a human being that shares eternity with God who created us. Of this world, we are also more than this world. Faith trusts in the existence of matching infinities, one outside of ourselves and one inside ourselves. Both are certain and central to faith.

EVIL AND MORAL MEANING

IF THERE IS a God, why is the world filled with such suffering and pain? Having clarified the religious view of human nature and its obligations, we can return to the question. The first question in the Bible is the one God asks Adam, "Where are you?" but as every believer knows, it can also be reversed "Where are *You*?" Where is God amidst all the anguish of this world?

"The Question of Evil" is usually phrased this way: If God is all good and all powerful, why would God permit suffering and evil? The most discussed question in religious history will find no new answers here, but we can synthesize two answers, both tied to our ultimate purpose in this world, in the hope that they will provide some guidance.

Religion has traditionally assumed that the aim and end of life is for human beings to grow in soul; the poet Keats called the world a "vale of soul-making." Growing in soul, to deepen our understanding, broaden our imaginations, and enhance our courage and compassion, can take as many forms as there are people; there is no single path. To grow requires that the world be so constructed to enable us to make choices. And the ability to choose requires free will.

FREE CHOICE

BEGINNING IN CHILDHOOD, everyone understands constraints. They are the necessary conditions of living. Much of our free will is, paradoxically, spent in denying ourselves and preventing others from making certain choices.

———

WHEN OUR DAUGHTER was born, we engaged in a new parental rite—we hired a baby-proofer. The baby-proofer

added gates, locks, and gizmos to keep our baby from get-
ting into trouble. Rough edges were smoothed with rubber
bumpers, dangerous passages blocked off with gates. After
all this work, and considerable cost, the baby-proofer turned
to me as he was leaving and said sternly, "Now remember,
you still can't let her out of your sight for a minute."

My daughter was constrained for her safety, but only a
bit. The same is true for us in the world. Certain things we
cannot do by physical limitation, such as run thirty miles
an hour. Other constraints we place on ourselves, such as
not driving one hundred miles an hour. There are infinite
degrees of choice and restriction. The very same gesture
may reflect dissimilar kinds of choice: When someone with
a gun asks us to lift our hands, our free will is limited. To
lift those same hands in prayer is a choice.

Belief in free will is the bedrock of religion. It is also the
bedrock of every sane person's functional thinking about
the world. No one speaks as if he has no choice in things as
different as choosing a shirt and selecting a mate. Choose
badly or well, they are equally sharp illustrations of free
will.

The argument against free will is elegant: No person selects her ancestry or selects, before birth, her environment.
Biology and family are destiny. Therefore, if there is nothing apart from genetics and environment, free will is indeed
hard to defend. When could free will possibly enter the picture? Evolutionary biologist David Barash says it does not:

"There can be no such thing as free will for the committed scientist." A materialist thinker assumes we possess as much choice as a rock rolling down a hill.

Materialism says no free will; all of our deepest instincts say we possess free will. For me, the contradiction is resolved by the recognition that free will is not contradicted by genetics, but gifted by God.

With God, choice is given; it is precisely the point of the enterprise of human life. Unprovable it may be; indispensable to life it surely is. One who turns to God may be inclined to follow the philosopher William James, who resolved that his first act of free will would be to believe in free will. James concedes there is no decisive argument that can turn this eternal debate one way or the other. All of our culture is built on the assumption of free will; it is the teaching of great religions that such will is God's paradoxical gift to us—to do good, or to do ill.

———

Free will is the capacity that permits human beings to foster goodness and inflict pain. Without choice there is no growth, just an endless repetition of obeyed, if unconscious, commands. A world without free will is a world of puppets or robots, not human beings. Yet this will is granted at a terrible cost. Regimes of systematic cruelty use free will to strip others of their free will. So much of the agony of the world is a result of free will that it feels at best an ambiguous gift.

Few would choose to be automatons, but the blessings of choice are woven throughout with the agony of misguided or cruel choices.

Humanly caused suffering is of course only a part of what human beings must endure. Disease and natural disasters have plagued our history, and there is no adequate answer to the anguish and death these have wrought. Part of the response of faith is to understand what role suffering might play in the way human souls grow.

When we ask why bad things happen to good people, we have to recognize the consequences envisaged by that question. Imagine good things always happened to good people and bad things always happened to bad people. Every time you robbed, you would be stricken with disease. True, you would never steal, but the choice not to steal would have no moral meaning. We would be like rats in a Skinner box, pushing the bar to receive a pellet of food. Morality in its highest form consists of being good regardless of what befalls us. To be good only to get something in return is not goodness, but expedience. If the aim of life is to grow in soul, goodness cannot be merely prudence.

Many of us might readily forfeit purity for goodness—let people get rewards, so long as they are good! But the best way to destroy goodness is to make it always dependent upon a reward. In education we begin by rewarding a student, but to get a lifelong learner we must cultivate love of learning itself. To get a reliably moral person there must be a commitment to morality that cannot simply be shaped by reward.

A program of simple reward and punishment destroys the intrinsic meaning of being good. Religious traditions have long known the perils of morality by reward, a conclusion newly demonstrated by psychology. Experiments demonstrate that children who are rewarded for playing games soon lose interest in the game itself. Those without the reward sustain interest in the activity. By rewarding behavior, we risk undermining it. Human beings respond to a very complicated and always shifting system; rewards and punishments matter, but they cannot be all. To do good is to do good without any certainty of reward. Achieving goodness in the world as a demonstration of soul growth is a crucial aim of all serious religious traditions.

An ancient rabbi notes that we see not through the light of the eye but through the dark of the eye. Pain is indispensable to growth. Once I was asked to address a group of recovering alcoholics. After the meeting, one of them approached me and said that he was now forty and had been sober for five years. He began drinking at sixteen, and when he stopped at thirty-five he still had the maturity of a sixteen-year-old. "You see," he explained, "from sixteen to thirty-five I was always drunk and felt no pain. Since I was never in pain, I never grew."

———

ANY PHYSICAL WORLD is an impermanent one. The reality of decay and death is built in to our world, since a cosmos composed of material, of "stuff," by its very nature cannot be perfect. I believe that there is a spirit, a Divine spirit in the world. The existence of spirit does not change the reality that the world through which it moves is physical and therefore perishable.

Free will, moral growth, and the reality of matter's impermanence are ways in which religious thinkers seek to understand evil. All of these considerations have helped me, but I know them ultimately to be inadequate.

EVIL—HOW MUCH CAN WE REALLY UNDERSTAND?

AT THE AGE of thirty-one my wife was diagnosed with cancer, leaving her, ten months after the birth of our only child, unable to bear more children. There are innumerable kinds of losses in life. One of them is the loss of potential, of what might have been. We mourned the loss of the children that would never be. We mourned the loss of certainty and security in the world, a loss that comes to all of us in time. We felt lucky to have our daughter and to have each other. Her experience was harrowing and heartbreaking. So long as she remained healthy, however, we thought it would be a challenge we would have faced and overcome.

Four years later I was delivering an address at the dedication of a building at my alma mater, the University of Pennsylvania. Earlier that day I had felt a little disoriented, feverish. While speaking, I noticed it was hard to keep my mind on what I was saying; I felt myself drift. I sat down after the talk and almost immediately had a grand mal seizure. Fortunately, some doctors were attending the talk; massive doses of tranquilizers finally stopped the seizure in the ambulance. Had it occurred in any of a dozen different places—from behind the wheel of a car or in the bathtub— I would have died.

Mercifully, I do not remember anything of the seizure itself. I was unconscious. From the moment I woke up in the hospital and for the next few days I was confused. I asked the same questions over and over. I saw people and an hour later forgot that I had seen them. The CT scan showed nothing. Upon returning from Philadelphia to my home in Los Angeles, my wife took me for an MRI. Looking at more precise images, the radiologist told us there was "an area of concern." For twelve hours that bland-sounding, terrifying phrase ran through our minds over and over. The following day we were told I was to have surgery to remove a lesion in my brain.

Two weeks separated the seizure and the surgery. During that time my wife told me I was not entirely myself. I did not make jokes; I was automated. I remember thinking that as I read I was somehow separated from the "me" that was reading. Like a character in an Oliver Sacks book, I became a dulled spectator of my own life. A religious attitude toward the world looks for the potential of blessing in pain. Was that possible through cancer, brain tumors, surgeries, seizures, fear, and misfortune?

Wondering what surgery on my brain might yield, I thought constantly about my mother's stroke and subsequent aphasia. I recalled the weeks of waiting while she was in a coma, the devastation an injury to the brain can produce. Over the years I watched my parents seek to negotiate simple tasks together, often with difficulty and always with frustration at the effort required to communicate.

Preparing for brain surgery I knew from my mother's experience what might happen. As I went under before the surgery, I said a prayer that I knew might be my last.

My first memory after the operation is of the surgeon standing over me, telling me it went well, but that there was still an 85-percent chance I would need radiation—perhaps one treatment, perhaps several. That is to say, the tumor was almost certainly malignant. Then the nurse offered me morphine. I told him no drugs until I saw my wife, because I did not want to be cloudy when I first saw her.

When Eliana walked in and I said hello, she told me later that she could tell instantly I was myself again. The nurse asked how bad the pain was, 1–10. I said about 5 or 6. Did I want one morphine capsule or two? I had never had morphine, and this was my chance: "Two," I said. My wife told him I was slight, and that he should start with one. "No, two," I reiterated. "Please—just start with one," she said. I turned to the nurse and said, "I made a mistake, I should have taken the morphine before I saw her!" All three of us laughed. That was when she knew for sure I was myself again.

The diagnosis came the following week; the tumor was benign. Now both of us would have follow-up scans forever, but we felt we had dodged two bullets.

Three years later, however, I was diagnosed with non-Hodgkins lymphoma. Unrelated to my previous illness, this was a new challenge and a different one. For there is, at present, no cure.

FAITH IN SHADOW TIMES

SITTING WITH THE needle in my arm, I revisited all the questions that tormented my teenage years. Did God exist, or care? Was faith an illusion, or just sometimes elusive? Now I was a rabbi. I thought I had resolved to understand what I could and leave the rest to a wisdom beyond anything I could imagine. In less than a single decade, shock after shock had upended our lives and I wondered anew about the source of faith, and of the question, "Why me?"

I HAVE NOTICED something interesting about that question. Rarely does someone come to my office to say, "Rabbi, I live in the wealthiest country in the world and have never gone hungry—why me?" Or, "You know, my parents were good, kind people and treated me with love—why me?" The blessings we receive we seem to accept as our due. Difficulties in life cause us to rail against the injustice of the world.

"We can be thankful," said the Roman philosopher Seneca, "to a friend for a few acres and a little money; and yet for the freedom and command of the whole earth, and for the great benefits of our being, our life, our health, and reason, we look upon ourselves as under no obligation."

———

A CANCER TREATMENT center has a strange effect on gratitude. There is usually no shortage of people who are in more severe straits: children, repeat patients back in hopes of a brief reprieve. Still, it is hard to feel grateful for being in a less dire condition than others, and the confusion of emotions inside of me came out in prayer. During moments when there are cracks in our complacency, prayer has room to slip in. The prayer was not that I be saved, but that God stay close—connection, not magic. Prayer meant more to me than ever, but still there was a nagging question: Was the relationship real or did religion come from fear?

As I was recovering, I began to read about a series of books being published that argued for atheism. In a renewed way, religion was a source of controversy. This was something I understood; these were arguments I knew. But approaching it now was unlike the intellectual journey of my youth. My cancer, and my wife's cancer, had not given me new information, but rather a new sensibility. Existence, the sheer, exhilarating fact of existence, is miraculous. I did not suddenly begin celebrating every sunset or cheering the coming of each dawn. I do not transcend the difficulties of life—a flat tire still irritates me and I still find a solicitor's phone call at dinnertime annoying. Life is not ideal, but for the moment, it is mine. I am alive.

I do not know about tomorrow, next month, or next year. After all, no one does. For now, I am in remission.

Why am I in remission? I heard this question as I began to hear all such questions, on two levels. One was answerable by reciting the cocktail of drugs that I had been given. The other was what purpose would be served in the world by the time I had been granted through that remission? This was not a scientific question but a religious one. In some sense, we are all in remission, all in a terminal condition, but I am now acutely conscious of it. As with great art or soul-stirring music, the awareness returned me to life's first principles. To feel one's own mortality certainly evokes fear that one will be gone, but also it evokes appreciation for all that outlives us. Sometimes knowing we can lose all we have helps us love those things—the sky, the stars, even God—that are beyond having.

———

OUR UNDERSTANDING OF ultimate questions is limited beyond even our understanding of the limitation. As theologian Milton Steinberg said: "The believer in God has to account for the existence of unjust suffering; the atheist has to account for everything else." I had no certain explanation of my illness, but I had one for the array of wonders that greeted me in this world. My questions were not all answered, but I felt, I feel, so enormously grateful to be able to ask them.

Responses that had become helpful to me such as the idea of soul growth, the randomness of reward to help ensure genuine goodness, the mutability of matter—all of them took a backseat to a greater reality. Questions of evil always required more explanation than anyone could give. Evil became for some the reason to abandon faith; for others it became the reason to confess to limitations of understanding.

Realizing how much I could never understand, for me the question of evil is less a "why" question than a "what" question. Not "Why does evil exist?" but "What can I do to make the world better?" Some years ago I wrote a book called *Making Loss Matter: Creating Meaning in Difficult*

Times about how to cope with loss in one's life—loss of home, loss of dreams, loss of faith, loss of love, loss of those we cherish. It was in the midst of writing it that my wife Eliana was diagnosed with cancer.

The writing of the book changed dramatically on the never-to-be-forgotten day we received the doctor's phone call. Suddenly all that I had taught was tested in my own life. I understood that the essential question of life was not why does this happen, which we can never fully know, but how do we create something powerful and lasting from our wounds.

In that book I recounted the stories of people who changed their lives in response to tragedy. For many it opened a path to a deeper engagement with others and a richer understanding of themselves and of the world. Since I completed that book I have seen countless other examples of such courage allied to faith. A woman in my congregation died of cancer, leaving three daughters who created a foundation in her memory that has contributed to breakthrough discoveries in the disease that claimed their mother's life. There is a hospice program at my synagogue for the care of the terminally ill established in memory of a man whose inspirational courage and resolute faith in his final days touched all who knew him.

There is a child in my congregation with diabetes whose reaction to the disease has been to become a national spokesperson for juvenile diabetes. Liza credits her struggle with the disease with helping shape her soul, and moving her toward the rabbinate, which is her professional goal in life.

Does such courage make undergoing the pain worthwhile? It depends upon the circumstances and the outcome of the trials each endures. Again and again it becomes not a search for explanation but a quest to respond. Faith in God reaches a new level. No longer is the promise that bad things can never happen. The promise is the strength and the faith to create meaning and beauty from loss.

We do not wish for suffering. The scale of pain in this world dwarfs, at times, any attempt at explanation. Not every prayer can be answered. But every soul can find solace in prayer.

THE PRACTICE OF PRAYER

LATELY THERE HAVE been scientific studies to establish the effectiveness of prayer. Such studies will always be inconclusive. You cannot measure the effect of prayer the way you measure the effect of sunlight. Nor is it like a slot machine, where sometimes you hit the jackpot and other times the investment is simply wasted. God may be supplicated but not coerced. The human task is not to tote up results, but to engage in this mysterious and beautiful discipline of the soul.

To judge prayer we cannot look at its results in the external world alone. In his lovely *Diary of a Country Priest*, the French novelist George Bernanos writes:

> The usual notion of prayer is so absurd. How can those who know nothing about it, who pray little or not at all, dare to speak frivolously of prayer? . . . If it were really what they suppose, a kind of chatter, the dialogue of a madman with his shadow, or even less—a vain and superstitious sort of petition to be given the good things of this world, how could innumerable people find comfort until their dying day . . . in the . . . sheer, robust, vigorous, abundant joy in prayer? . . . Could a sane man set himself up as a judge of music because he has sometimes touched a keyboard with the tips of his fingers?

———

DEEP PRAYER IS an experience like music or love —indescribable to one who does not pray. Prayer works through you. To be carried away is to be in prayer. To be expressively in touch with something greater is prayer. Prayer is not the same as poetry; prayer is directed to God. I may read a poem and glory in its imagery; when I recite a prayer I am grateful for having been heard.

A seventeenth-century rabbi, Leona Medina, explained it this way: If you watch a man out on a boat grab a rope and pull his boat to shore you might think, if you were confused about weight and motion, that he was really pulling the shore to his boat. People have much the same confusion about spiritual weight and motion: In prayer, some believe that you are pulling God closer to you. But in fact the heartfelt prayer pulls you closer to God.

I have prayed in fear and in joy, in crisis and in calm. Each time I understood that what I was asking for was not the object of my prayer. My prayer that I would be healed was a prayer, stripped of all its topmost layers, to be assured that whatever happened would be all right. Every prayer in this way is a prayer for peace; it is peace in the world and in one's soul, the certainty that the pain is not empty, the world not a void, the soul is not alone.

Prayer can ultimately be judged only by its effect on the one who prays. Communication between human beings is so subtle and various and uncertain, we should not expect that when an individual or a community opens itself to God we can chart the result on a graph.

THE VALUE OF TRADITION

"How much have you seen, eh, theiflet? Africa, have you seen it? No? Then is it truly there? And submarines? Huh? Also hailstones, baseballs, pagodas? Goldmines?

Kangaroos, Mount Fujiyama, the North Pole? And the past, did it happen? And the future, will it come? Believe in your own eyes and you'll get into a lot of trouble, hot water, a mess."

Salman Rushdie, *Haroun and the Sea of Stories*

SOME PRAYER IS a spontaneous overflow of the heart, and other prayer is part of a long-established liturgical tradition. Tradition exists not only in prayer, but in virtually every area of life; religion brings home to us what is true in the rest of our lives as well—most of what we know is a legacy of others.

The world is so vast and various that no one can know firsthand more than a slice of reality. We believe we know far more than we experience ourselves. Tradition, that musty, slightly suspect notion, is the indispensable carrier of knowledge, glimpses of what has been passed down but lies beyond our direct experience.

Religion leans heavily on tradition. The central stories and ideas of faith, however, are those handed down for generations.

These tales are about the experience of the Divine entering human life. God's presence is felt in a new and powerful way. This experience yields new ways of living in the world. Love, decency, fraternity, law, goodness, charity—these were known long before any of the religions we cherish. Each was given a new dimension, a higher and deeper expression, in the traditions of the great faiths.

Therefore, religious stories are about more than the past, they are about the present. The Divine once entered the world. That experience can be created anew through ritual. Religious rituals recapture the moment when heaven and earth met. In religious traditions, pivotal events do not happen once. They are always happening anew in the life of the believer. The Exodus recurs in the life of a Jew; for a Christian, the resurrection, for a Moslem, the hagira. Holidays and traditions speak about the history not only of the world, but of the recurrent history of the human soul. This is the journey each person takes in the world, they tell us. Redemption is not an historical event but a present reality.

The salvational stories of faith do not tell only of what was—they are about what is.

Religious stories conflict even within traditions. Truths about human beings are not singular, but various. Clichés about life contradict each other too: absence makes the heart grow fonder, and also, out of sight out of mind. He who hesitates is lost, and we should look before we leap. Religious traditions speak in many voices because many voices, multiple truths, live inside human beings.

Literalists may argue that every word of every story is strictly factual. A deeper view of guiding religious stories is that even when they are not factual, they are true. The deep stories of tradition capture essential truths that are more profound than literal accuracy. From homespun parables to tales of the miraculous, they are encouragements to spiritual sight, teaching that one who sees only what is visible misses much of life.

IMPROVING GOD'S WORLD

DOES RELIGION MAKE people better? Do believers in fact take on that challenge to improve the world?

Listen to the most famous of the Enlightenment thinkers, the French philosopher Voltaire:

"I want my attorney, my tailor, my servants, even my wife to believe in God because then I shall be robbed and cuckolded less often."

Voltaire's conclusion is that people who believe in God will be more honest. Would you expect it? Does religion indeed make more ethical individuals, ones less likely to cheat, steal, and betray?

The emphasis on goodness that is so prevalent in religious traditions is a restraining hand on cruelty. Yet it has to do battle with the very powerful inclinations in human beings to do wrong. Ivan Karamozov famously declares in Dostoevsky's novel that without God everything is permitted. Given the savagery of which human beings are capable, what will they do if there is no overarching standard and guide? Where is the grounding of morality without supernatural sanction? I may be inclined to be helpful, but when it is against my interest, why should I?

Along with countless religious educators I have had the dispiriting experience of trying to get teenagers to say why they should be good if it is not in their interest. Why leave a tip in a restaurant you will never visit again? I have watched them struggle with this simple example; none was sure he could offer an adequate answer.

For the believer there are both sanctions and deeper motivations. The belief in reward and punishment is certainly effective in the short term. (Are you more likely to observe the speed limit with a police car behind you or not?). But there is also the deep conviction that God wants us to be good. Goodness arises from fidelity to God and from love to one another.

Religion is hardly a foolproof test of morality. A nonbeliever may be equally kind, giving, and heroic. A building may stand strong with a rickety foundation, but for society in general, belief has a long-lasting effect on moral behavior. Absent such belief, morality will continue for a while, but can it endure? As one philosopher put it, ethics are like a cut flower, fragrant only for as long as it can sustain the nourishment of the soil from which it was plucked.

Even when religions conflict, there remains a powerful motivation to care for the other man's faith. J. David Bleich, a noted Jewish scholar, once wrote of his experience in Eastern

Europe: "My great-grandmother said, 'When you are riding in a horse and wagon and pass the door of a church, if the driver does not cross himself, get off immediately.'" Even with the antagonism between the two faith communities, this bit of folk wisdom assumed that no faith was far more dangerous. Without belief, moral behavior has no set standard. Believers violate their own standards all the time; without a faith tradition is there even a set standard to violate?

We have all watched religious figures disgrace themselves and their traditions through immoral or unsavory conduct. Religious miscreants encourage those who argue that religions are hypocritical and empty. Yet one can make precisely the opposite case. The only reason such conduct outrages us, apart from our usual sad sigh at the misdeeds of human beings, is that we really do expect more from religious people. Devoutness feels real to most of us. When it is violated, the offense is somehow greater than normal hypocrisy or cruelty. Religion creates a moral climate that alters, to varying degrees, the behavior of believers.

If human beings are accidents, there is no standard above our desires. Further, no cross-cultural standard exists to which all can appeal. We may have ethical intuitions, but are they more than preferences? The prevailing law of animals is that the stronger survive. In the jungle, you cannot be both strong and wrong. That you can in fact be more powerful and still be wrong is, on the other hand, a linchpin of religious ethics.

One who does not believe in God may be an outstanding individual, but that person can be a monster with equal intellectual consistency. For if we are all products of accident, animals in evening coats, then our actions have no more need of moral justification than the lion or the wolf.

> Why should men love the church? Why should they
> Love her laws?
> She tells them of Life and Death, and of all that they
> Would forget.
> She is tender where they would be hard, and hard
> Where they like to be soft.
> She tells them of Evil and sin, and other unpleasant
> Facts.
> They constantly try to escape
> From the darkness outside and within
> By dreaming of systems so perfect that no one will
> Need to be good.
> But the man that is will shadow
> The man that pretends to be.
>
> (T. S. Eliot, "Choruses from
> 'The Rock'")

Religion can be a comfort, but also an affliction. As Eliot's poem expresses, religion reminds us of things we would rather ignore, or forget.

Religious traditions are filled with exactions that would have no place if the stakes were not souls. "Sin," "evil"—these words sound harsh, unwarranted to modern ears. We know how easily they are abused, exploited to describe things that are hardly sinful, and certainly not evil.

But are there not genuine evils in this world? Have we not some sympathy with the title of the 1973 book by humanistic psychologist Karl Menninger, *Whatever Became of Sin?* The discourse of good and evil, of right and wrong, which is still sorely needed in our world (perhaps more than ever), sometimes to condemn the very evils of religion itself, derives from religion.

At times people avoid religion not from lack of faith, but because they cannot face up to the consequences of faith in their own lives. God can be the Creator of the world and I will rest undisturbed; as soon as God is the Creator of my own soul I have obligations to live a certain way. Acknowledging God as *my* God, I can never be the same.

THE AFTERLIFE

WE MAY SPEND our lives searching for justice in this world, and seeking to foster it. Still, from our earliest expressions when we indignantly protest to our parents, "It's not fair!" we know how unfair the world can be. As the

Book of Job says in an evocative image, the evildoer dies old and blessed "with his pails full of milk" (Job 21:24). Too often the reverse is also true; the righteous live difficult, even tragic lives.

This should not startle us unless there was reason to expect justice. We do not call bacteria that invade our body evil. They may be unwelcome, painful, and powerful, but they are not evil. Justice is the expectation of a creature who intuits a perfect order. Only those who think life *should* be a certain way attach values to facts and see illness or suffering as evil.

Understanding evil, righting evil, is the most powerful and painful dilemma in religion. Since this world is unfair, and since we do have a vision of a worthy world, faith traditions have wondered about the reality of an afterlife.

Religions propose that this world is not all. Theology and instinct persuade them that there is something beyond this life. But we have no experience of that world. Despite chronicles of near-death experiences and people who believe they have died and returned, the science in this can never be decisive. The very idea that there is another world offends many people's common sense.

Could anyone imagine this world before she entered it? Who would be able to think of mountains and tuna fish and eyes and plants and buildings and books before experiencing them? Similarly, when we try to envision another world, it is always this world with a twist. We cannot really imagine that which we have no experience of at all. Our ideas are elaborations of things we already know. So when we think of what another world might be, we fall headlong into foolishness. In *Letters from Earth* Mark Twain writes that people assume that after they die they will lie on verdant fields and listen to harp music. We wouldn't want to do that for five minutes while we are alive notes Twain, but we assume that it will keep us happy for eternity after death.

Imagination does better with pain than with bliss. Dante's *Inferno* has always seemed to me a more successful poem than his *Paradiso* because pleasure is so fleeting and hard to grasp but pain is concrete and easy to imagine. So the torments that religion describes are horrible and easy to project. The rewards seem ephemeral and often silly.

The essential affirmation is anything but silly, however. It joins two ideas: that we have a responsibility to establish justice in this world and that eternity can correct what time leaves uncompleted. There is a Divine economy; it takes place, as does the earthly economy, in a very different sense, by means of an invisible hand.

A parable asks us to imagine twins lying together in the womb. Everything they need is provided. One brother believes, "irrationally," that there is a world beyond the womb. The other is convinced such beliefs are nonsense. The first tells of a world where people walk upright, where there are mountains and oceans, a sky filled with stars. The other can barely contain his contempt for such nonsense.

Suddenly, "the believer" is forced through the birth canal. Imagine how the brother left behind must view this—a great catastrophe has befallen his companion. Outside the womb, however, the parents are rejoicing. What the brother left behind has witnessed is not death, but birth. This is a classic view of the afterlife—it is a birth into a world that we on earth cannot begin to imagine.

OCCAM'S RAZOR AND BURIDAN'S ASS

RELIGION TEACHES ONE more unprovable but essential belief. Perhaps it is best approached by way of a rhetorical device that has been made to bear much more atheistic freight than it can really carry.

Several anti-theistic books appeal to Occam's razor, a rhetorical principle teaching that entities or assumptions should not be multiplied beyond necessity. It is named after William of Occam (c. 1285–1349), an English Franciscan friar and philosopher. Occam's razor is used to propose, for example, that in theorizing about the creation of the world, if one can account for it without a Creator, so much the better. Your philosophical checkbook is balanced. Not a cent wasted.

Actually to expel God requires a bunch of other assumptions. While Darwinism supposes that the less complex frequently grows more complex, as single-cell organisms make their way up to become prodigies like Johann Sebastian Bach, to suppose that complexity arises in physics may not work so easily by analogy. Imagining the universe came from nothing might be far more complicated, and require many more assumptions, than to believe something outside the universe got it started.

So Richard Dawkins writes: " . . . however little we know about God, the one thing we can be sure of is that he would have to be very very complex and presumably irreducibly so!" This is a startling example of applying the laws of physical beings, and indeed physical beings that have evolved on earth, to God. If God were a biological creature like the possum or the crawfish, Dawkins would have a sound point. But here biology is doing the work of theology. The argument for the unity of God, which was formulated in different ways by all the great medieval theologians, was intended precisely to prove that God is an intangible unity, not a complex or compound organism.

So Occam's razor, as intended by Occam himself, can actually do the work of faith. Throughout the centuries many educated and unlettered people have been able to understand the idea that God created the world. It might be in many ways the less complex idea.

Here is a strange contradiction: To believe in God, we are told, is simultaneously too simpleminded and too complex.

It is far easier and economical to believe the universe arose without a guiding intelligence. Yet it is also simpleminded to believe in a guiding intelligence. In other words, religious people are too unsophisticated to realize that the belief they hold is too intellectually complex for the problem.

In place of Occam's razor I would like to propose that the key medieval parable for our time is Buridan's ass.

Jean Buridan (1300–1358) was a French priest. His name became attached to a parable that apparently pre-dated him, but no matter. It still speaks to us and is worth remembering.

To put this in context recall how often the "god" of reason is invoked in writings by rationalistic anti-theists. "Reason," Sam Harris tells us in *The End of Faith*, "is the guardian of love." More, he writes, "I know of no society in human history that ever suffered because its people became too reasonable." Hitchens writes " . . . we distrust anything that contradicts science or outrages reason."

Now reason is an invaluable tool. Without it, nothing, including faith, can flourish. But reason alone is not only dangerous but virtually impossible. Such is a ringing truth brought to us by Buridan's ass.

Imagine a donkey equidistant between two barrels of hay. Now imagine that this donkey is a rationalist, someone who will do nothing if it is not in accord with the dictates of reason. He cannot reason why one mound of hay is superior to the other. He stays in the middle trying to decide which should be his supper. Since there is no reason to move to one or the other, in time, the donkey starves to death.

Obviously Buridan's ass is a parody, although a parody with serious intent. In making fun of philosophers, Buridan was teaching that reason bleached of value starves us. Reason does not give us a reason to live, to get up in the morning, to improve the world, to help another who will not be able to return the favor. Reason is a powerful tool to accomplish ends that are established by means other than reason. The neurologist Antonio Damasio has demonstrated that when people who suffer brain injuries that destroy their capacity to feel seek to make decisions, their decisions are disastrous. Reason alone, unaided by emotion, by vision, is a poor compass to navigate this world.

When Leviticus counsels "love your neighbor as yourself" (Lev. 19:18), it is not a counsel of reason, but a command of faith. The world needs reason, but reason alone will doom the world. To fashion a reason that will help us survive, the world needs God.

CARING FOR CREATION

WE ARE RESPONSIBLE for this world. Stewardship of the planet is an urgent spiritual task. Perhaps the world began in a garden, but since then we have both planted gardens and uprooted them. Our capacity to fashion the world to our needs is impressive and ultimately, if we are unwise, could be apocalyptic.

In the story of Noah, God offers humanity a rainbow and a promise that God will never again destroy the world. What is *not* promised is that humanity will not destroy the world. That verdict remains to history—and to us.

Reading the Bible

"The Scriptures cannot be understood but by the same spirit that gave them forth."

Emerson

AT SEVENTEEN YEARS old, a week after my childhood synagogue moved to a new location, I went back to visit the now deserted sanctuary. The electricity was off. The building was cold, fixtures stripped, and walls bare. Light streamed through the stained glass windows onto abandoned seats. Scattered about were torn pages from prayer books and bibles. Standing in front of the empty ark, I sorted through the texts and found a page with the verse that opens the biblical book of Lamentations: "How does the city sit solitary, that was full of people!" Slowly and sadly, I turned and left.

For years that sentence was the story I told myself about losing my faith. Once the sanctuary was filled; now it was vacant. The eternal light above the ark was out; the pulpit was barren, the seats would be ever empty.

The passage from Lamentations epitomized my experience. The bleakness of a desolate room reflected what I was missing inside.

Ironically it was the Bible that expressed my loss of faith. I had seen so much that was wrong with the world that the magic enchantment I felt in my youth had long since fled. The city, for me an image of the protected world of God's care, now sat solitary. Each of us was alone. The Bible itself gave voice to all my uncertainties.

The Bible is not written for one era or generation. It has survived because it speaks anew to each receptive spirit, in each successive age. When I first learned the stories of the Bible they were interesting, at times charming. With age they deepen into comfort, inspiration, and provocation.

In the years since that time, I have found in the Bible an ever-renewable resource for meaning and guidance. Approached with cynicism or skepticism, sections of the Bible can seem cruel or incomprehensible. Approached as a sincere attempt to puzzle out God's will in this world, filled with missteps and startling truths, the Bible can prove—as it does in my life and the lives of countless millions—to be a book that shines a light on our souls.

THE BIBLE IN LIFE

MANY TIMES I have sat by the bedside of someone who is sick and read the Psalms. Psalms are the personal prayers addressed to God, often by one who is in trouble or peril. They act as a remarkable channel for the anxieties and hopes of one who is ill.

When the time came for me to be the one in the bed, not beside the bed, I turned to the same source: Knocked out by the chemotherapy and unable to carry on the usual tasks of the day, one verse kept recurring in my mind, Psalm 118:5. It is usually translated "from out of the depths I called unto God; He answered me and set me free." But the "depths" can be translated as "narrowness" and free as "expansively." A literal translation is—"From my narrowness I called to God and I was answered by breadth, O God." My world grew through pain and the increasing recognition of the ways in which it both opened my heart and helped me draw closer to others in pain. A single verse offered a world and way of seeing that gave me strength and the breadth promised by the verse itself.

My spirit opened to an infinitely larger Spirit. When in pain, we tighten up like a fist. It is easy to push others away—after all, they are not feeling the pain—and to turn increasingly inward. Only I matter; only my pain is real. The Psalm urged me to expand, allowing me to embrace others, to understand that pain need not always be private, unshared. Open up, the Psalmist taught; both in heaven and on earth you are not alone.

The Psalmist also connected my pain to the human community throughout the ages. Thousands of years ago a poet gave words to what was deep within me. A hand reached across the generations to take my own. That, too, seemed like more than just a human gift; it was a gift from God.

———

BIBLICAL SUFFERERS TOUCH us through their shared pain. In our fractured and difficult lives, reading a chronicle of difficulty and failure can be encouraging and even healing. The heroes of the Bible are not perfect; their marriages are not storybook, their relations with children not frictionless. All of us who struggle with real problems of families, of work, can look to the Bible not as one looks at a fairy tale, but with the recognition that everything has changed since the time of Abraham and Sarah except human nature.

GREAT READERS

WALT WHITMAN WROTE that in order for there to be great books there must be great readers.

For a book to remain powerful throughout generations it *cannot* have a single meaning. Scripture, like great poetry, is not reducible to other words; that is, one cannot paraphrase it and capture the totality of its meaning. "Yea though I walk through the valley of the shadow of death I will fear no evil" simply does not mean the same thing as "even if I come close to dying I am not worried that something bad will happen." The words, particularly in their original Hebrew, contain nuances and resonance that go beyond any attempt to simplify them. T. S. Eliot was once asked by a woman the meaning of the following line in his poem "Ash Wednesday": "Lady, three white leopards sat under a juniper-tree." Eliot's response was "Madame, what the line means is 'Lady, three white leopards sat under a juniper-tree.'" Eliot must have known that any explanation of meaning would make the line less than it was, so he resisted all explanation. Interpreters of scripture, understanding the infinitude of meanings, take the opposite approach from Eliot. Instead of refusing to interpret, they never stop.

Nor do the commentators always read the Bible literally. For example, the militarism of the Bible's language has not been taken at face value. The exhortations to conquer the land of Israel did not incite violent plots or wars throughout the middle ages.

Those who decided that settlement and, if necessary, armed conflict would restore the Jews to their land were the early Zionists, very few of whom were religious. In other words, those Jews who took the Bible most literally were not themselves observant Jews. And those who most revered the Bible did not read it literally. When war broke out, religious communities were vastly underrepresented in the army. Rather, those who were far more influenced by secular society—while nourished by the biblical vision of the Jews resettling in their land to be sure—were the ones who ended up fighting.

If you read only the Bible you would not expect such a result. The secularists should be the pacifists and the traditionalists should be the ones prepared to fight. That the reverse is true tells us something we already know—the Bible offers different messages depending upon the care with which it is read and upon the reader's approach.

Another example of how the Bible must be read in the context of the culture is offered by Matthew 10: 35–36: "For I have come to turn a man against his father, a daughter against her mother, a daughter-in-law against her mother-in-law, a man's enemies will be the members of his own household."

Someone who reads this verse in isolation will assume that Christians have very poor family relations. Moreover, they will assume that it is considered laudable by Christianity to have poor family relations. I have yet to find a serious interpreter who believes the desire of Jesus in this passage is to cause families to fall apart. Many contend that it is a sometimes sad and inevitable result of one following a path of faith of which others disapprove. Whether that is the correct interpretation matters little. What does matter is that all traditions agree that in order to read scripture there must be some understanding of the overall intent of the Bible. With the question of war above and family here, the Bible is not *Bartlett's Familiar Quotations*, a place where a single verse can be isolated from all that precedes and follows it. The Bible both reflects the culture in which it is read and helps shape that culture. One sentence is no more reflective of the whole Bible than one gesture is of an entire personality.

At times it appears religion's detractors believe nothing in the Bible except for accounts of cruelty. But in order to understand any book or any idea we have to see what it means as it is reflected through lived lives, through an individual's and a people's journey.

HOW DID THEY JUDGE THE BIBLE?

HOW DID ANCIENT readers judge the Bible? The answer is—by the Bible.

Let us take the infamous verse of the rebellious son of Deuteronomy chapter 21. The Bible instructs parents of a gluttonous, drunkard, disobedient son, who will not listen to his parents, to declare his rebelliousness before the community and stone him as punishment. The ancient rabbis, whose entire lives were defined by immersion in the biblical text, could not abide the idea that a parent could be responsible for the stoning of his own child. They knew quite well that in ancient societies children were routinely stoned and sacrificed. The idea that parents would never put their own children to death is contradicted by the ancient world as well as innumerable dynastic struggles where family was often the first to be killed.

But the rabbis were conditioned by the morality of the Bible itself. Other cultures did sacrifice children but not those shaped by scripture. When confronted with the question of a rebellious child, the Talmud unambiguously states, "A rebellious son (as defined by the Torah) never was and never will be."

The Bible's most devoted readers understood that the Bible as a whole forbids the savagery of children being stoned for disobedience. So they declared it should not be taken literally. For the Bible was then as now to be understood as a guide to God's goodness in this world. Those sections that seemed to contradict such a reading were considered improperly understood, and had to be reinterpreted to enhance the Bible's message of holiness.

Among the most notorious of all the troublesome passages in the Bible is the narrowly averted sacrifice of a child. The binding of Isaac (a more accurate name than "the sacrifice of Isaac" since Isaac indeed lives) is one of the most commented-upon stories in biblical history. In the twenty-second chapter of Genesis, God calls upon Abraham to take his son up to an altar and offer him as a burnt sacrifice. Abraham gets up early in the morning, walks three days with his son, climbs with him up the mountain, binds him, and lifts the knife when he is stopped just in time by an angel. This story, reflected in the story of Jesus in the New Testament (carrying the cross as Isaac carried the wood up the mountain, each about to be sacrificed) and retold (with changes) in the Koran, is central to all the Western monotheistic traditions.

Christopher Hitchens adverts to it as follows: "There is no softening the plain meaning of this frightful story." Richard Dawkins in his book *The God Delusion* elaborates, "By the standards of modern morality, this disgraceful story is an example simultaneously of child abuse, bullying in two asymmetrical power relationships, and the first recorded use of the Nuremberg defence. 'I was only obeying orders.'"

Let us leave aside that Abraham never makes any such claim or feels the need to do so. What strikes me is Hitchens's almost offhand comment leading up to his condemnation of this story: "Before monotheism arose, the altars of primitive society reeked with blood, much of it human and some of it infant." Just so. That infamous practice ended with monotheism, and the binding of Isaac tells us how it happened.

The story is about the willingness of a believer to admit that the One who created all can ultimately decide the fate of everything in the created world. Abraham is not by nature slavish or cowardly; in a previous chapter he vigorously argued with God to spare the inhabitants of Sodom, who have no moral claim on him save that they are fellow human beings (Gen. 19). But he takes Isaac to the altar. In this he acted as did all the pagans around him, showing that this new God, the real God, the intangible God whom one cannot see or carve of stone, can command the same devotion as the ancient pagan gods. He does this only to learn, however, that while his passion is honored, the action is not permitted. The true God would not claim such a sacrifice. As both ancient and modern scholars of the Bible explain, the story teaches that one does not need to offer the ultimate sacrifice to feel the ultimate sense of devotion.

Sacrifice is at the heart of religious ideology. It can be perverted into cruelty or a misguided martyrdom. But it can equally prove to be the mainspring of goodness and nobility. It is instructive to hear Bertrand Russell and Martin Luther King Jr., an atheist and a preacher, respectively, on the willingness to be sacrificed. When asked in an interview once if there is anything for which he would be willing to die, Russell wryly answered, "Of course not. After all, I may be wrong." King, on the other hand, said, "A man who won't die for something is not fit to live." Sacrifice is not about a foolish willingness to give up one's life, or the life of another, for oppressive ideology; that is simple tyranny. Sacrifice is the belief that one has duties to the world that go beyond simply existing in it.

———

THE BIBLE PRESSES upon us core issues of life, which we too often choose to evade: the relation of parents and children, what we cherish and what we sacrifice, whether there are ideals for which we are willing to give our lives. Reading the Bible moves us to deepen our lives by reflecting on ultimate issues. Part of the resistance to religion, and to the Bible, is that it entails grappling with profound questions. It is unlike any other book; not only eternal but urgent, a book that returns us to the world more alive to its wonder and more compassionate for its pain.

WHO WROTE THE BIBLE?

SOME UNDERSTAND THE Bible as collaboration, as a record of how human beings experienced God. For others it is the literal word of God. In no case is it the only path to knowledge of God.

God speaks through nature, including human nature and through history as well as through scripture. Science helps us understand God by unraveling the subtleties of nature. Sociology and history help us understand God by looking at patterns through time. Psychology and art illuminate human character and experience. Scripture enables us to understand the way in which these insights can contribute to the Divine mandate to live with compassion and seek peace.

———

IN THE PAST few hundred years, biblical criticism has challenged the idea that the Bible is the literal word of God. Powerful arguments have been advanced based on new techniques of analyzing texts and other discoveries from archeology and social sciences. Whatever one's conclusion, reading the Bible can still be an experience unlike any other in literature. It is simply not equivalent to reading Gilgamesh and Homer, Milton and Shakespeare. The Bible speaks from a particular historical moment, but also from beyond the ages. As I experience this with the Hebrew Bible so does the Christian with the New Testament and a Muslim with the Koran. For thousands of years people read the Bible with a deep sense of wisdom imparted and peace granted. They returned to it, as millions across the world do today, again and again, knowing that there was more to understand than they had yet understood.

Strange and powerful sections of the Bible, rather than being candidates for ridicule, are opportunities for insight. Such possibilities may not unfold to the casual reader and indeed there are things that take a lifetime to understand. Quite often, different understandings of the book are appropriate for different stages of life. For much of the world the Bible calls to mind what the Greeks said of Plato—whatever road of life you walk down, you find him on the way back.

To take one example: Several of the anti-theistic works ridicule the final commandment "Thou shalt not covet." It is reckoned tyrannical because one cannot legislate emotions. In the Hebrew Bible the famous commandments are not termed commandments but sayings (*Devarim*). That permits a nineteenth-century rabbi to explain it as follows: Thou shalt not covet is not a command, but a promise. Observe the other nine and you will live a life that is not wracked by desire for things you cannot have. You will be at peace with what you were given. Once again the Bible yields wisdom and serenity when approached not as an "ordinary book" characterized by what Sam Harris calls "obscene celebrations of violence" but as a guide through the obstacles of life. The Bible can be mocked, just as all seriousness and insight can be mocked. The mockery does not advance the skills we need to live; cynicism makes a good sword but a poor shield.

ANTHROPOMORPHISM

PHILOSOPHER DANIEL DENNETT writes that some believers think that to ask questions like "Does God have eyelids?" is to be insulting. Meaning no disrespect, I don't find it disrespectful. It is simpleminded, however. People who pledge allegiance to the physical world may not appreciate that everything nonphysical requires metaphors. The

Bible's descriptions of God are not intended literally. To ask if God has eyelids is as sensible as asking if kindness has a pancreas.

There is no escaping physical description; in talking about spiritual matters we use words taken from the physical world, as Ralph Waldo Emerson observed in his essay "Nature":

> Every word which is used to express a moral or intellectual fact, if traced to its root, is found to be borrowed from some material appearance. *Right* means *straight*; *wrong* means *twisted*. *Spirit* primarily means *wind*; *transgression*, the crossing of a *line*; *supercilious*, the *raising of the eyebrow*. We say the *heart* to express emotion, the *head* to denote thought; and *thought* and *emotion* are words borrowed from sensible things, and now appropriated to spiritual nature.

God communicates with human beings, so we speak of God having a mouth. God shows love, so we speak of God having a heart. Faith is the reality that can only be spoken of in poetry.

The Bible's poetry encourages us to see the world in supermundane—more than material or physical—terms. Religious perception is a poetic faculty, keeping alive within us the reality of a world that cannot be understood by logic or reason alone. "The heavens declare the glory of God," writes the Psalmist (Ps. 19), encouraging us to see the stars as conveying something of the grandeur and beauty of the world. They do not literally speak, of course, but the world has been reenchanted through the poetry of faith.

THE BRIGHT BOOK OF LIFE

THE BIBLE TELLS of carnage, cruelty, inexplicable evil. In part this is because the Bible is in fact what D. H. Lawrence called the novel—the big bright book of life. Everything is here: Stories of heroism and pettiness. Selfishness and deceit. Desperation and triumph. It is not always clear what derives from the dark heart of humanity and what is a teaching from God.

———

UNDERNEATH THE TUMULT is the lived reality of God. Through warfare and family relations, lawgiving and discipleship, inspiration and disappointment, the current of God's will pulses through the lives of biblical characters. The Bible presents God but does not seek to "prove" God. Faith is not a proposition but an orientation to the universe, a certainty that accompanies the characters through their days and nights, and if he is fortunate, accompanies the reader as well.

Recall the first time childhood friends made an observa-
tion about your family. Or perhaps when you were married and your spouse began to tell you what your family of
origin seemed like to her or to him. Some of their observa-
tions were eye-opening. You never noticed before how your
mother shut down when asked personal questions or how
your father's reminiscences did not correspond with your
own. But at the same time, there were things you could not
explain that you understood: why your sister was treated
differently by your parents, or the undercurrent of love beneath apparent conflict.

Why is your understanding different? It is not only because you are part of the family. Being raised in the family
has given you a perspective that cannot be achieved from
the outside.

Those who read the Bible inattentively do not understand
that the Bible equips its readers with the means to understand it. To read through it once is not to know it. Immersion allows a new kind of understanding. The same is true of
religious systems: one can't evaluate them on first acquain-
tance. Tourists visiting a foreign country easily find flaws or
oddities: The way people eat, the food they serve, their dress
or speech, or their child-raising techniques may seem alien
and unorthodox. In time, however, one begins to see it with
different eyes. Theory gives way to experience. Knowledge
becomes personal. We can only see with our own eyes.

Not even science, contrary to what many think, strips away this subjectivity. As the chemist and philosopher Michael Polanyi notes, all knowledge is inevitably personal knowledge. Knowledge gets filtered through individuals, all of whom were brought up in a certain family, culture, language, and place. There is no perfectly objective view. Religious traditions do not just offer propositions to evaluate by the light of reason. To embrace a tradition is to stand in a new place. Each of us brings to the tradition our own matrix of understanding and the tradition alters and colors it, creating something new. Standing inside a tradition, the world looks different. To call it simply "true" or "false" is to reduce a world view to a multiple-choice exam.

As a junior in college, I spent a year in Scotland at Edinburgh University. One of the first days of walking to class there was a small, steady drizzle. I did not yet know that there was almost always a small, steady drizzle. I grabbed an umbrella and started on my way.

The Scottish students with whom I walked, once they stopped laughing, ripped the umbrella from my hands. They explained that the drizzle was simply part of the world, and soon would be part of my world. Only an outsider would carry an umbrella.

Naturally I thought that was ridiculous. Rain, after all, is rain. Wet is a fact. You cannot pretend wet is dry—at least not if you are sane.

But I was new and wanted to be liked, so I went along. Sure enough, in a short time I was walking with everyone else and not noticing the rain. It had become part of the world in which I lived, and seemed natural.

There are two ways to see this sort of experience. I could be sadly deceived—these Scottish rakes fooled the naïve American. Or you could imagine that in fact the world began to look different because I was given new eyes. Reality did not change, but my understanding of it and adjustment to it changed. I was not now "wrong" when I had been "right."

When we read the Bible, there are some passages that sound savage to our ears. Still, a lot depends upon how we are taught to read the Bible, and whether we allow the Bible's own voice to condition our reading. What seems at first wild and fraught proves to be a window through which we can take the measure of our own world. We have to decide how the Bible fits in our lives; as the Scottish poet Andrew Lang said about facts, some people use them as a drunk uses a lamppost, more for support than for illumination. You can find much in the Bible to support any reading of it, but if you read it for illumination, the world changes.

The Talmud tells of an idolator who is interested in converting to Judaism. He approaches the Rabbi Shammai with the request that the rabbi teach him Judaism while standing on one foot. Shammai, believing that he is being mocked, or his faith belittled, chases the man away. The same man then approaches Hillel. Hillel lived more than half a century before the birth of Jesus, and he spent his life immersed in the Bible and rabbinic interpretations.

What for this rabbi is the essence of the tradition? Here is his response: "What is hateful to you, do not do to your fellow. That is the whole of Torah—the rest is commentary. Now go and learn."

With all we hear about the presumed cruelty and barbarity of scripture, how could someone whose entire life was the Bible answer in such a way? Where did Hillel learn that this was "the *whole* of Torah"? Hillel is one of the two or three greatest authorities of the rabbinic period. This is the word of a great sage who did not read simply a sentence or story or pluck at random from a sacred text, but lived the full text. Even the greatest book relies on being read with an understanding heart. Hillel demonstrated what the book can mean.

One who reads the characterizations of the Koran, similarly, may not realize that the five pillars of Islam are belief, prayer, giving (tithing to the needy), fasting, and pilgrimage. The test will always be how the book plays out in life. For Jews, Christians, and today most poignantly for Muslims, the measure of meaning for scripture will be the way in which its adherents act in the world. Whatever gifts God gives us have value in life only as they are filtered through a human soul.

The Bible is preeminently a book about righteousness. Again and again we hear concern for the widow, the orphan, the one who is bereaved, bereft, hopeless, alone. No one can say the Bible is meaningful to them if they do not feel a mandate to lessen poverty and alleviate suffering. When the prophets criticize Israel it is in the name of Israel that they speak—what Israel should be, what faith demands. For all the assaults of unbelievers, the ones who are hardest on the faithful are the faithful, for the world sorely needs passionate goodness, and we so often fall short.

———

MORE THAN THIRTY years have passed since I left the empty synagogue sanctuary of my youth. I thought I was closing the door forever on its teachings. A part of me needed to do just that; faith seemed too childish and I thought myself an adult.

Even more, I could not truly come to faith until I had left. The Bible was to me a fairy tale because I had not lived long enough to catch up with some of its teachings. Coming to it anew years later, having lived, having accumulated some scars and drawn close to others who were far wiser than I, the words of the prophet appeared as a challenge to me, explaining what God asks of us: "To do justice, love mercy and walk humbly with your God" (Mic. 6:8). Decades after walking out of the sanctuary, I have grown to believe faith enables us to do this, and so I have gratefully returned.

SEVEN

Is Religion Good for You?

"This mountain is such, that it is always hard at the start below, and the higher one goes the less it hurts."

Dante, *Purgatorio*

THE TRUTH OF religion is not proved by its helpfulness. Religion may be good for you and still not be true. Religion may create a more stable society, a happier person, a more secure family, and still rest on illusions. One must wonder why believing falsehoods would prove to enhance human life, but it is at least possible. But *is* it good?

———

MORE STUDIES THAN the reader would have patience for demonstrate that religion is indeed not only very good for the people who practice it, but for society as a whole. Religious people are happier, more charitable, have more stable families, and contribute more to their communities. One of the best ways to understand whether religion is beneficial is to look at people who once were not religious and who became religious. Did it help their lives?

Consider, for example, this remarkable testimony by Professor Armand Nicholi Jr.:

> Several years ago I conducted a research project exploring Harvard University students who, while undergraduates, experienced what they referred to as a 'religious conversion.' I interviewed those students as well as people who knew them before and after their conversion. Were these experiences an expression of pathology, i.e., isolating and destructive, or were they adaptive and constructive? Did these experiences enhance or impair functioning? Results published in the *American Journal of Psychiatry* stated that each subject described a "marked improvement in ego functioning [including] a radical change in lifestyle with an abrupt halt in the use of drugs, alcohol, and cigarettes; improved impulse control with the adoption of a strict sexual code demanding chastity or marriage with fidelity; improved academic performance; enhanced self-image and greater access to inner feelings; an increased capacity for establishing 'close, satisfying relationships;' improved communication with parents, though most parents at first expressed some degree of alarm over the student's rather sudden, intense religious inter-

est; a positive change in affect, with a lessening of 'existential despair;' and a decrease in preoccupation with the passage of time and apprehension over death."

———

STUDENTS AT HARVARD may improve the quality of their lives through religion, but what of the rest of us? The *Wall Street Journal* cites the 2004 General Social Survey. It tells us that religious people were twice as likely as nonreligious people to say they were "very happy." Not only were they happy at the moment, but they were a third more likely to be optimistic about the future. This is an important variable in an age in which studies also demonstrate how critical optimism can be to stability and a productive life.

The 2000 Social Capital Community Benchmark Survey showed that practicing Protestants, Catholics, Jews, Muslims, and people from other religions are all far more likely than secularists to say they are happy. Those who identify with faith but practice inconsistently are generally happier than secular people, but not as happy as regular practitioners.

———

AN ARTICLE FROM the *London Sunday Times*, June 4, 2000, written by Dr. Raj Persaud, Consulting Psychiatrist at the Maudsley Hospital in South London begins: "Want to live longer? Medical research from the National Institute of Healthcare Research in America suggests you might be better attending church than going to the gym." The study notes that religious people (even with all the cholesterol-clogging church picnics) have lower blood pressure than the nonreligious. Says psychologist Dr. Michael McCullough, the lead author of the study: "The odds of survival for people who rated higher on measures of public and private religious involvement were 29% higher than those people who scored lower on such measures."

You might suppose that all of this benefit is a result of community. But it is difficult to build lasting community apart from religious institutions. The country club to which you belong may disappear, your reading group disband, the bowling club close. But faiths will endure.

Community alone is not enough; faith is a powerful addition to the communal spirit. The same *Sunday Times* article cited above continues:

> But science also finds support for the idea that religious involvement is helpful beyond the more mundane benefits of group support. For example, recent research on Israeli kibbutzim, which are usually cohesive supportive communities, established that living in more religious kibbutzim was associated with considerably lower mortality than secular ones.

LINDA GEORGE, SOCIOLOGY Professor at Duke University, writes:

> As all of you know, there is now strong evidence that religious involvement is associated with a variety of positive health out comes including delay in the onset of physical and mental illness, better course and outcome of physical and mental illness, and longer survival. Among the multiple dimensions of religious experience, attendance at religious services is the dimension of religious involvement most strongly related to health and survival.

What has she learned from the "thousands of older adults who have participated" in her studies? "Most importantly they have taught me that quality of life is at least as much a function of what we believe as what we have."

A common charge against religion is that it puts blinders on its adherents. Yet the meaning that religion grants is not rigid or narrow but something broader and more beautiful. Commenting on the wealth of studies showing a link between religion and happiness, Dr. Barbara Fredrickson of the University of Michigan says: "Perhaps what is distinctively human about our emotional lives then is our ability to open our minds far enough to fathom or create a connection to God, or another Higher Power. This broadened mindset can in turn provide a wellspring of profoundly experienced emotions, many of them positive."

————

DR. HAROLD KOENIG of Duke University summed it up as follows:

> The benefits of devout religious practice, particularly involvement in a faith community and religious commitment, are that people cope better. In general, they cope with stress better, they experience greater well-being because they have more hope, they're more optimistic, they experience less depression, less anxiety, and they commit suicide less often. They don't drink alcohol as much, they don't use drugs as much, they don't smoke cigarettes as much, and they have healthier lifestyles. They have stronger immune systems, lower blood pressure, probably better cardiovascular functioning, and probably a healthier hormonal environment physiologically—particularly with respect to cortisol and adrenaline [stress hormones]. And they live longer.

Twelve-step programs can aid those who are in trouble. The second step, of course, is to acknowledge there is a higher power and to establish the right relation to God. Belief does not only help those who are in relatively good shape, but lifts those who are in the depths, and helps set them free. Such faith-based healing is not part of an organized religious program (although organized religions run their own addiction programs as well) but demonstrates yet again the force of allowing transcendence—or, God by another name—into one's life.

In an age when we are beset by family breakdown, faith can help shore up declining social confidence and capital. Consider these findings:

Research shows marriages in which both spouses frequently attend religious services are 2.4 times less likely to end in divorce than marriages in which neither spouse worships. In fact, researchers at Duke University Medical School found that religious attendance is *the most important* predictor of marital stability.

One study discovered that men who attend religious services at least weekly were more than 50 percent less likely to commit an act of violence against their wives than were peers who attended only once a year or less.

W. Bradford Wilcox of the University of Virginia found that a father's religious attendance was positively associated with his involvement in activities with his children, such as one-on-one interaction, having dinner with his family, and volunteering for youth activities. In fact, fathers' frequency of religious attendance was a stronger predictor of paternal involvement with their children than employment and income—the factors most frequently cited as pivotal.

Arthur Brooks of Syracuse University highlighted the robust relationship between religious practice and charitable giving. In a general survey population, religious individuals were 40 percent more likely than their secular counterparts to give money to charity and more than twice as likely to volunteer.

Eighty-seven of over one hundred studies reviewed concluded that religious practice is significantly correlated with reduced incidence of suicide and depression.

Research further shows that, as Pat Fagan, author of the study "Why Religion Matters Even More: The Impact of Religion on Social Stability," explained in a recent interview, "The single biggest new finding was the effect of religious practice on the poor. There is an intriguing indication that they benefit more than those with more income, and benefit significantly." Religion's impact on the poor is especially compelling on outcomes related to drug use, academic progress, and juvenile delinquency.

In one study of young males from impoverished inner-city Chicago and Philadelphia, for instance, researchers found that a high level of religious attendance was associated with a 46-percent reduction in the likelihood of using drugs, a 57-percent reduction in the probability of dealing drugs, and a 39-percent decrease in the likelihood of committing a non drug-related crime.

Fagan's research demonstrates that, on an entire range of outcomes—from domestic abuse, educational attainment, and marital stability to substance abuse, violent crime, and even immigrant assimilation—the practice of religion is a powerful predictor of personal well-being and societal stability.

Finally, the *Los Angeles Times* reports that researchers found that people without faith are less likely to register to vote (78 percent versus 89 percent) and less likely to help a poor or homeless person (41 percent versus 61 percent) even though they are more likely to be college graduates and have higher income than believers. Americans of no faith typically contributed $200 a year to charities; active-faith Americans $1,500 a year. Even when church-based giving is subtracted from the equation, active-faith adults donated twice as many dollars a year as atheists and agnostics. This accords with a recent study by the Barna Group, which conducts research for Christian ministries. The Barna Group concluded that religious Americans give seven times as much to charity on a per capita basis as do nonreligious Americans.

Religion will not make us perfect or guarantee a conflict-free world or an easy life. In fact, religion can make life considerably less comfortable when it pushes believers to do more than they would otherwise do. Some who travel to impoverished areas of the world, tend to those who are sick, or raise awareness and money for important causes would live easier lives if they did not believe they were doing God's work. Such activities can also bring happiness, because such service is uplifting to those who believe it is sacred.

Here is the judgment of Carl Jung, one of the preeminent students of human nature in the preceding century:

> During the past thirty years, people from all civilized countries of the earth have consulted me . . . Among all my patients in the second half of life—that is to say, over thirty-five—there has not been one whose problem in the last resort was not that of finding a religious outlook on life. It is safe to say that every one of them fell ill because he had lost that which the living religions of every age have given their followers, and none of them had really been healed who did not regain his religious outlook.

———

ON BALANCE, RELIGION increases social stability, enabling people to live happier, more charitable, more productive and better lives. That does not demonstrate religion's truth. It does remind us, however, that we are creatures designed to flourish—to heal and to help—when we believe.

EIGHT

Why Faith Matters

"I am that I am."
Exodus 3:14

EVERYTHING THAT HAS been said in favor of religious faith is true of religion at its best. Too often religion shows its worst face to the world, as a mask for privilege or power, fanaticism, or manipulation. No institution touched by human hands is free from corruption. In our own day, as weapons become more potent, it is not possible to deny the potential of religion to do great harm if its adherents are triumphalist and ignore its messages of peace.

In my synagogue we often host groups and clergy of other faiths. When we do, it is remarkable how striking are our theological disagreements but how equally remarkable our human consensus. Our areas of disagreement are far less than our areas of concord: how we should treat one another, the limits of human knowledge and the reality of human ignorance, the need for God, the importance of human effort and seeking, and also the hubris that gets in our way. I live in Los Angeles, which is a powerfully multicultural city. The key to coexistence is not sameness but recognition of something greater than all of us.

CAN WE PROVE GOD?

ALL RELIGIONS HAVE a conviction in the rightness of their own tales and interpretations. Sensible though my faith may be to me, or yours to you, ultimately it is unprovable. The same is true on a larger scale of the enterprise of "proving" the existence of God.

For years I have taught Jewish philosophy to undergraduates in seminaries and universities. The beginning of the course covered the history of religious philosophy in general; we marched through all the proofs that have been given for God. I detailed the ontological proof, the teleological proof, the cosmological proof. Chalk in hand, I diagrammed each on the blackboard, explained the steps, the objections, the answers, the conclusions. Never, in more than a decade of teaching the course, did a student come up to me after class, clap his hand to his forehead, and exclaim: "Aha! Now I believe!"

Marilynne Robinson writes in her stark, powerful novel *Gilead*: "So my advice is—don't look for proofs. Don't bother with them at all. They are never sufficient to the question, and they're always a little impertinent, I think, because they claim for God a place within our conceptual grasp. And they will likely sound wrong to you even if you convince someone else with them."

Each day my life is touched by experiences that have nothing to do with proof. The music of my daughter's laugh, the thrill of reading a profound thought, a quiet moment at home with my wife. Who can prove that these are important? Who would wish to prove it? The deepest experiences of life are not the fruit of reason but of love.

If we rely on reason alone to prove something that is, by definition, beyond all human reason, we are back at the dream of Aquinas. The story is told that toward the end of his life this greatest of Christian theologians had a dream. In it, he was trying to empty out the ocean with a teaspoon. When asked by a student what he was doing in the dream, Aquinas replied ruefully, "theology."

———

THE OBJECT OF a believer's testimony is not proof. Religious traditions offer avenues to introspection, to compassion, and to faith. When I discovered the explosive potential of questions—questions I was prepared to follow wherever they might lead—the world opened up. The purpose of this book has been to clear away the cynicism, to suggest that the usual objections to faith—that science disproves it, that it is dangerous, that it is irrational—are simply not true. It has also served, I hope, to show that in questions, in reverence, in the words that Buber spoke, "all real living is meeting," lies the possibility of meeting the living God. Not a God on a page, or a God of ancient miracles. Not the God of this or that faction, or the God who is invoked on coins and in campaigns. Rather the living God who whispers inside us, the powerful force urging us to goodness and giving us a sense of peace. This God cannot be proven or disproven. This God, who can be intuited, can be felt, is the living God. And this God can never be argued away.

WHY ARE WE HERE?

"A man had been wandering in the forest for several days unable to find a way out. Finally he saw another man approaching. He asked him 'Brother, will you please tell me the way out of the forest?' Said the other, 'I do not know the way out either, for I too have been wandering here for many days. But this much I can tell you. The way that I have gone is not the way.'

So it is with us. We know that the way we have been going is not the way. Now let us join hands and look for the way together."

Rabbi Hayyim of Zans

HAVE WE LOST our way? Even though we have some sense of where we should go, we find society spinning off in dangerous directions. In seeking one another, in joining hands, we may find a new way.

In our time, the violence of fanatics, murder in God's name, has persuaded some that religion has led us astray. Such fanaticism is not a product of belief, but of the insecurity of belief. The renowned theologian Reinhold Niebuhr wrote, "Frantic orthodoxy is never rooted in faith but in doubt. It is when we are not sure that we are doubly sure." Such fanaticism does not present a viable direction for the survival of the world, but neither does untrammeled scientific discovery that cannot alone govern or direct itself. Only faith that understands human frailty and human nobility, that believes holiness is not separate from compassion, points us to the path out of the wilderness.

What are we here for? The Darwinian answer to this question is that we are here to make more of us; reproduction is the end of life. We are here so that we can remain here. We do not know anything beyond that.

Religion, on the other hand, answers that question on a different, deeper level. We are here to grow in soul, to achieve goodness, to work for causes larger than existence alone. Righteousness and devotion are the expressions of a life of sanctity.

Being here so that we can reproduce is a paltry, inadequate explanation for human existence. It is an answer without a vision. Such an answer makes all of human society, the struggles, the achievements, the interpersonal connections, into an elaborate breeding farm. The principal objection to this is not that it is uninspiring, though it is that; the principal objection is that it is untrue.

———

I LOST MY faith when I first encountered the horrific images of the holocaust in the documentary *Night and Fog*. Over the years I began to understand that faith was both bigger and smaller than my rejection. Bigger, because it was about how everything came to be. It told the tale of life's balance and complexity. While my doubts were not new, many before me had found the faith—even in the camps themselves—to feel God despite terror and pain. Smaller, because to know God was not only to ask momentous questions of good and evil, but to delight in the everyday wonders of God's world. Simple gestures and quiet awakenings often overwhelm doctrine and metaphysics. Years later, when I began to read the Holocaust literature in depth, I found a vivid, disturbing passage that brough these themes back to me.

Perhaps the most terrifying moment in all the literature of the Holocaust is in Primo Levi's masterpiece *Survival in Auschwitz*. Recounting his time in the camp, Levi recalls that while suffering from thirst he broke off an icicle out-side a barracks window. When a nearby guard "snatched" it from him, Levi asked, "Warum?" "Why?" The guard responded in German, "Hier ist kein warum" "Here there is no why." The greatest terror is if the universe presents a blank face—if, as in the camp, there really is no why.

If there is no God, there is no why. Faith believes in the legitimacy of asking "why"—that the very question is an animating force in life.

I began this book beside the bed of a man dying of cancer. He wanted to know why. It brought me back to the losses in my life, to the question that hovered above them, the question that never leaves us. Why? Why did my mother lose her voice? Why did my wife have cancer? Why did I have a brain tumor, lymphoma? Why have I watched so many good people suffer? Why, why? The difference between the world as I know it and the world Levi portrays is not that I can answer why, but that I can answer there *is* a why. I reject the nihilism of nothingness. God is not the automatic answer to all questions, but the assurance of meaning.

———

THERE IS NO single way to summarize the message of faith. But perhaps a story can help; it is a tale of the recov-ery of the oldest bit of scripture known to us, more than 500 years before the birth of Jesus, more than half a millennium older than the next oldest fragment, the Dead Sea Scrolls.

Some years ago Israeli archaeologists came across this remarkable discovery. Just outside the walls of Jerusalem, the
archaeologists found the burial cave of a family. We know
that this family had survived the destruction of the First
Temple by the Babylonians in 586 BCE because the artifacts
in the cave were dated from fifteen years after the Temple
had been burnt to the ground. Perhaps even more remarkable, their tomb had not been pillaged by grave robbers in
the intervening centuries.

The grave was in the valley of Hinnom—Gehinnom—
the valley that became for Jews a very powerful symbol.
This was the valley where pagans sacrificed children, and in
Judaism "gehinnom" is the word for hell.

When they cleared away the debris, the archaeologists
found, among the pieces of pottery and household objects,
two amulets in the form of tiny silver scrolls, just a few
inches long. Crusted with dirt and corrosion, they had been
rolled shut for 2,600 years.

Working with painstaking care, opening them gently and
slowly, they found a barely legible inscription, the oldest
parchment of any piece of sacred scripture that exists.

The tiny amulets read: "May God bless you and keep
you. May God cause His countenance to shine upon you
and be gracious unto you. May God turn His countenance
upon you and grant you peace."

A blessing for peace had been snatched from destruction,
from the midst of hell on earth.

The radiance of faith endures throughout the centuries. Our task is to ensure that faith holds within it a promise of peace.

WHY FAITH MATTERS

"God does not die on the day when we cease to believe in a personal deity, but we die on the day when our lives cease to be illuminated by the steady radiance, renewed daily, of a wonder, the source of which is beyond all reason."

Dag Hammarskjold

GOD'S REPUTATION IN this world is in our hands. When religious pluralism turns to religious intolerance and brotherhood to bloodshed, it is God whose name is diminished. When conviction turns to bigotry and service is service only to one's own community, God's name is diminished.

In a series of debates around the country and online I will have the chance to answer specific criticisms of religion. I did not clutter this book with a rebuttal of every charge or a riposte to each clever remark. We do not always learn by debate. As a friend of mine told me years ago, his life changed when his wife said to him, "You know, you can win the argument and still be wrong!"

——————

PERHAPS THE GREATEST philosopher of the modern age, Immanuel Kant, famously wrote that two things filled him with awe, the starry heavens above and the moral law within. Strangely in our day, both have waned in our awareness. We block out the starry heavens with the lights of our cities, and we block the moral law within by belittling the idea that it originates from beyond us, calling it a trick of the times or a contrivance of evolution. But even when we cannot see them, both wonders exist. People come to God through the majesty of the world, and the messiness of their lives.

The future of God will depend in part on our own openness. Inside of most human beings, perhaps all, there is a capacity for faith. But embarrassment or mockery can blunt the chance for reverence.

——————

THERE ARE MOMENTS in every life when suffering or difficulty opens the way for understanding. It has been true in my life, and no doubt will be again. I have not reached a final understanding of anything discussed in this book, and never expect to. Still, the darkness does not only obscure, it also clears a path for the receptive soul.

At the dedication of the Jerusalem Temple, King Solomon said (1 Kings 8:12): "The Lord has said that He would dwell in a dark cloud." Faith has not only moved those of us whose life is filled with understandable gratitude. Many have found God precisely in the suffering that one might assume would chase all thoughts of the Divine away. From Boethius writing Christian philosophy in jail in the sixth century, to Anatoly Sharansky clinging to a book of Psalms in a Soviet prison camp, great testaments to the power of spirit have come through darkness. Those who oppose religion might see this as delusion or desperation. But naysayers on the outside of such faith-forged perseverance should not belittle those who have endured and overcome. It may be, it just may be, that their belief provided strength not because it was convenient, but because it was true.

The questions that moved me to write this book also led me to faith. I began to understand that questions about science, history, evil, tragedy, mystery, were all questions that could open doors. Some questions had answers beyond what I could know. In our time, from this tiny corner of the world, a fraction of a fraction of the known universe, clever men deduce that there is no God. Others among us, perhaps less clever but no less clear, feel certain that there is, and that our lives are immeasurably better for believing it.

Why does faith matter? Love of this world, of one another, is the sole hope in an age when we can destroy the world many times over. There is no power that is only good, that cannot be twisted for evil. Religion is hardly an exception. But while there are many things that can doom us, only one thing can save us. Faith. Not blind or bigoted faith, but faith that pushes us to be better, to give more of ourselves, to see glimmers of transcendence scattered throughout our lives. Such faith is both an achievement and a gift: It is an achievement of seeking, questioning, yearning, reasoning, hoping, and it is a gift of God, who fashioned this world, whose goodness sustains it and whose teachings could save it if only we—believers and deniers both—would listen, would love.

ACKNOWLEDGMENTS

THANK YOU TO those who helped this book along in various ways: Dan Adler, Rebecca Begin, Joseph Epstein, Nicole Guzik, Victor Davis Hanson, Melvin Konner, David Myers, Larry Weintraub, and Ron Wolfson; my father and brothers, Gerald, Steve, Paul, and Daniel Wolpe; my wife Eliana and my daughter Samara.

The prelude appeared first in a different form in *Moment* magazine.

A special thank you to three people who worked tirelessly to help me refine and improve this work: David Black, Abigail Pogrebin, and Claire Wachtel. Finally thanks to the clergy, staff, and congregants of Sinai Temple for all their support.

Works of Jewish piety traditionally end with the Hebrew phrase *Tam V'nishlam, Shevah L'el Borei Haolam*: Finished and complete, praise to God who fashioned the world.

NOTES

CHAPTER 1: FROM FAITH TO DOUBT
Page 5. On Bertrand Russell:
> Bertrand Russell, *Why I Am Not a Christian* (George Allen & Unwin, 1967), 26.

Page 16. On Douglass Hofstader:
> Douglas Hofstader and Daniel Dennett, *The Mind's I* (Basic Books, 2000), 6.

CHAPTER 2: WHERE DOES RELIGION COME FROM?
Page 26. On Richard Dawkins:
> Richard Dawkins, *The God Delusion* (Houghton Mifflin, 2006), 174.

CHAPTER 3: DOES RELIGION CAUSE VIOLENCE?
Page 46. On Gibbon's theory of Rome's fall:
> Edward Gibbon, *The History of the Decline and Fall of the Roman Empire* (Folio Society, 1997), 373.

Page 47–48. Nietzsche on morality:
> Friedrich Nietzsche, *Geneology of Morals and Ecce Homo,* trans. Walter Kaufmann (Vintage, 1967), 33–34.

Page 50. On the world without religion:
> Lawrence Keeley, *War Before Civilization: The Myth of the Peaceful Savage* (Oxford University Press, 1996).

Page 52. On the rule of the world:

   Thomas Gray, "Elegy Written in a Country Churchyard."

Page 55. On the Spanish Inquisition:

   See Henry Kamen, *The Spanish Inquisition,* (Yale University
   Press, 1998), chapter 9.

Page 57. On causes of the Hundred Years' War:

   John P. McKay, *A History of Western Society, Fourth Edition*
   (Houghton Mifflin, 1991), 362.

Page 58. On the First Total War:

   David Bell, *The First Total War* (Houghton Mifflin, 2007),
   362. The population of England is charted in Paul Langford's
   A Polite and Commercial People: England 1727–1783, (Oxford
   University Press, 1998), 146.

Page 58. On the people's revolution:

   Michael Burleigh, *Earthly Powers* (Harper Perennial, 2007), 97.

Page 59. On despotic power:

   Adam Thorpe, review of *The First Total War,* by David Bell,
   Guardian U.K., August 11, 2007.

Page 64. On Germany without Christianity:

   Heine quoted in Burleigh, 443.

Page 67. On Holocaust survivor Viktor Frankl:

   Viktor Frankl, *The Doctor and The Soul* (Knopf, 1982), xxi,
   cited in Ravi Zacharias, *Can Man Live Without God* (Thomas
   Nelson, 1994), 25.

Page 68. On Christopher Hitchens:

   Christopher Hitchens, *God Is Not Great* (Twelve Books,
   2007), 247–249.

Page 69. On male mortality due to violence:

   Prof. Azar Gat, letter to *Times Literary Supplement,* September
   27, 2007, 6.

Page 69. On the disappearance of the Neanderthal:

Ronald Wright, *A Short History of Progress* (Anansi Press, 2005), 36.

Page 71: On how we stand in nature:

Elizabeth Arthur, *Island Sojourn* (Harper & Row, 1980), 188–189.

Page 72. On British philosopher John Gray:

John Gray's words can be found at www.bryanappleyard.com.

Page 75. On unreported social good:

Michael Shermer, *How We Believe* (Holt, 2003), 71.

Page 75. On Exodus imagery:

Michael Walzer, *Exodus and Revolution* (Basic Books, 1986).

Page 75. On New Testament ethics:

Saint Simon cited in Burleigh, 227.

Page 76. On clergy courage:

Ian Buruma's comment, the *Los Angeles Times,* September 29, 2007, A23.

Page 77. On a passage in *God is Not Great*:

Hitchens, 60.

Page 78. On critic Terry Eagleton:

Terry Eagleton, *London Review of Books,* October 19, 2006.

Page 79. On physicist Freeman Dyson:

Freeman Dyson, *The New York Review of Books,* June 22, 2006.

CHAPTER 4: DOES SCIENCE DISPROVE RELIGION?

Page 84. On John Calvin:

Calvin cited in Alister E. McGrath, *The Foundations of Dialogue in Science and Religion* (Blackwell, 1998), 124.

Page 85. On science and religion:

Lewontin quoted in Kenneth Miller, *Finding Darwin's God* (HarperCollins, 1999), 186. See Leon Wieseltier in the *New York Times Book Review,* February 19, 2006: "Scientism, the

view that science can explain all human conditions and expressions, is a superstition, one of the dominant superstitions
of our day; and it is not an insult to science to say so."

Page 86. On the science and religion war myth:

Stephen Jay Gould, *Rocks of Ages* (Ballantine, 1999), 83.

Page 87. On the National Academy of Sciences statement:

National Academy of Science, http://www.nasonline.org/site/
PageServer.

Page 87. On historian Diarmaid MacColluch:

Diarmaid MacColluch, *The Reformation: A History* (Viking,
2003), 661–663.

Page 90. On whether or not we have minds:

For Eccles views, see *Evolution of the Brain: Creation of the Self*
(Routledge, 1991).

Page 91. On dreams:

Selzer cited in Mario Beauregard and Denyse O'Leary, *The
Spiritual Brain* (HarperOne, 2007), 112.

Page 93. On evolution and faith:

Gould from "Impeaching a Self-Appointed Judge" available at
the Gould online archive, http://www.stephenjaygould.org/
reviews/gould darwin-on-tIial.html.

Page 93. On professor of biology, Ken Miller:

Miller, 283–284.

Page 94. On the discovery of the genome:

Francis S. Collins, *The Language of God* (Free Press, 2006), 107.

Page 96. On author's grandfather and Mr. Einstein:

The story of my father and Mr. Einstein first appeared in
Conservative Judaism, vol. 52, Fall 1999, 67–69.

Page 97. On saving someone one doesn't know:

On this topic there is a burgeoning literature; for an overview
see Marc Hauser, *Moral Minds* (Ecco, 2006), and Michael S.
Gazzaniga, *The Ethical Brain* (Ecco, 2005).

Page 99. On scientists' faith:

David Sloan Wilson, *Darwin's Cathedral: Evolution, Religion and the Nature of Society,* cited by Jared Diamond in *The New York Review of Books,* November 7, 2002.

Page 100. On disbelief in accidental life:

Paul Davies, *God & The New Physics* (Touchstone, 1983), 167–168.

Page 100. On chance in the universe:

The Bennett calculation is reported in *TLS,* June 1, 2006, "Haunted Technology" by Phil Baker.

Page 100. On the six numbers of the universe:

Rees, 4. Page's calculation is reported by William Lane Craig in J.P. Moreland and Kai Nielsen, *Does God Exist* (Prometheus Books, 1993), 143. Stephen M. Barr, *Modern Physics and Ancient Faith* (Univ. of Notre Dame Press, 2003), 129 ff.

Page 101. On the idea that the world is finely tuned for life:

Collins, 73.

Page 102. On a man facing a firing squad:

William Lane Craig in Moreland and Nielsen, 144.

Page 103. On Thomas Nagel's confession:

Thomas Nagel, *The Last Word* (Oxford University Press, 1997), 130–131.

Page 105. On the West's technological superiority:

Newton's views are discussed in John Brooke and Geoffrey Cantor, *Reconstructing Nature* (Oxford University Press, 1998), 34.

Page 105. On Robert Jastrow:

Robert Jastrow, *God and the Astronomers* (W. W. Norton, 2000), 116.

Page 106. On the laws of physics:
> Paul Davies, "Taking Science on Faith," the *New York Times*, November 24, 2007.

CHAPTER 5: WHAT DOES RELIGION REALLY TEACH?
Page 124. On how the universe created our planet:
> Wheeler is cited in Owen Gingerich, *God's Universe* (Belknap, 2006), 40.

Page 129. On no free will and the scientist:
> David Barash's free will comment can be found at http://www.humannature.com/nibbs/03/dcdennett.html.

Page 131. On reward and punishment:
> The experiment with children is reported in Alfie Kohn, *Punished by Rewards* (Houghton Mifflin, 1999). The entire book is an elegant elaboration of the idea that rewards often destroy motivation and prove to be counterproductive.

Page 141. On prayer:
> George Bemanos, *Diary of a Country Priest* (Carroll & Graf, 2002), 103–104.

Page 142. On confusion about prayer:
> Modena is cited in Marc Saperstein, *Jewish Preaching* (Yale University Press, 1989), 93–94.

Page 145. On Voltaire:
> Voltaire cited in James Q. Wilson, *The Moral Sense* (Free Press, 1993), 219.

Page 153. On Richard Dawkins:
> Dawkins, 125.

Page 154. On Sam Harris:
> Sam Harris, *The End of Faith* (Norton, 2004), 190.

Page 154. On Hitchens:
> Hitchens, 5.

Page 155. On Antonio Damasio:

Antonio Damasio, *The Feeling of What Happens* (Basic Books, 2000).

CHAPTER 6: READING THE BIBLE

Page 164. On the rebellious child:

Babylonian Talmud, Sanhedrin 71a.

Page 165. On Christopher Hitchens:

Hitchens, 206, and Dawkins, 242.

Page 166. On willingness to be sacrificed:

Bertrand Russell's words are given in Clifton Fadiman, *The Little, Brown Book of Anecdotes* (Little, Brown and Co., 1985), 483.

Page 169. On Daniel Dennett:

Daniel Dennett, *Breaking the Spell* (Viking, 2006), 206–7.

Page 173. On Michael Polanyi:

Michael Polyani, *Personal Knowledge* (University of Chicago Press, 1974).

Page 174–175. On Shammai and Hillel:

Shammai and Hillel story, Babylonian Talmud, Shabbat 31a.

CHAPTER 7: IS RELIGION GOOD FOR YOU?

Page 178 – 179. On Armand Nicholi Jr.'s testimony:

Armand M. Nicholi J., "A New Dimension in Youth Culture," *American Journal of Psychiatry*, 131:396-401, 1974, recounted in Nicholi, *The Question of God* (Free Press, 2002), 80.

Page 179. On the Wall Street Journal's survey:

Wall Street Journal, "The Ennui of Mother Theresa," September 30, 2007. Online at http://www.opinionjournal.com/extra/?id=llOO10672.

Page 179. On the Benchmark survey:

Benchmark Survey, available online at http://www.hks.

harvard.edu/saguaro/communitysurvey/docs/survey instru-
ment.pdf. The *Journal* article cites both the Benchmark and
General Social Surveys.

Page 181. On Linda George:
Linda George: The Annual George Maddox Lecture at the
Center for the Study of Aging and Human Development.

Page 182. On Harold Koenig:
Harold Koenig: http://www.beliefnet.com/story/190/story
19034 1.html.

Page 184. On Pat Fagan:
From Pat Fagan's report "Why Religion Matters Even More:
The Impact of Religious Practice on Social Stability" cited
in Human Events: http://www.humanevents.com/article.
php?print=yes&id=20776.

Page 185. On *L.A. Times* article:
The *Los Angeles Times* article appeared June 16, 2007. The
Barna Group study and related studies are available at www.
barna.org.

Page 186. On Carl Jung's judgement:
Carl Jung, "Psychotherapists or the Clergy," *Collected Works,*
vol. 11. Many more studies that support the conclusions in
this chapter are cited in Keith Ward's *Is Religion Dangerous?*
(Wm. B. Eerdmans, 2007). Cf. Jonathan Haidt in *The
Happiness Hypothesis* (Basic Books, 2006), 88: "Religious
people are happier, on average, than nonreligious people."

CHAPTER 8: WHY FAITH MATTERS
Page 188-189. On Marilynne Robinson's novel:
Marilynne Robinson, *Gilead* (FSG, 2004), 179.

Page 192-193. On Primo Levi's masterpiece:
Primo Levi, *Survival in Auschwitz* (Collier, 1961), 25.